THE NORTH CAROLINA MUSEUM OF ART

The First Fifty Years
1947–1997

A SELECTED CHRONOLOGY

by Peggy Jo D. Kirby

The North Carolina Museum of Art
The First Fifty Years, 1947–1997
A SELECTED CHRONOLOGY

EDITOR: **VIKI BALKCUM**
DESIGNER: **DEBORAH LITTLEJOHN**
PHOTOGRAPHERS (except where otherwise noted): **GUS A. MARTIN, RICHARD
E. EVANS, WILLIAM DEPALMA, GLENN M. TUCKER, SADIE J.
BRIDGER, LYNN P. RUCK, WILLIAM M. GAGE,
AND KAREN MALINOFSKI**
PHOTOGRAPHIC RESEARCH ASSISTANT: **WILLIAM HOLLOMAN**
EDITORIAL RESEARCH ASSISTANT: **MICHÆL KLAUKE**
COPY EDITOR: **JUNE SPENCE**
EDITORIAL ASSISTANTS: **BECKY BOOKER AND DALE PIXLEY**
PRODUCTION ASSISTANT: **KIM BLEVINS**

Printed on UV Ultra and Evergreen Papers by Carter Printing, Richmond, Virginia

First Edition © 1997 NORTH CAROLINA MUSEUM OF ART, RALEIGH

ISBN 88259-976-3
Library of Congress Catalog Card Number: 97-66026

CONTENTS

This publication was made possible with generous grants from

Burlington Industries Foundation

The Mary Duke Biddle Foundation

and gifts in honor of

Ann B. Turner
by her son, Frank J. Turner
and
Mrs. Charles M. Reeves, Jr.
by her daughter, Suzanne Reeves McKinney

The North Carolina Museum of Art gratefully acknowledges this support.

PREFACE

The story before you is a tale of North Carolinians who were willing to invest their time, energy, and resources — first in an idea, then in the realization of an institution that educates, enlightens, and inspires all who pass through its doors.

The history of the North Carolina Museum of Art also involves compelling tales of political courage — of progressive leaders who employed their highest diplomatic and oratorical skills to create for this state one of the finest collections of art in the Southeast.

The North Carolina Museum of Art gratefully acknowledges the contributions of those who have served it, both in public and in private life, and have brought it to the threshold of the next half-century. We who are now dedicated to continuing the traditions of excellence which distinguish your museum invite you to explore this story of its past — and welcome you to share its future.

INTRODUCTION

One of my great privileges in public service has been the personal association with many of the people influential in the formidable enterprise of creating and shaping the North Carolina Museum of Art. From Robert Lee Humber, Katherine Pendleton Arrington, William Valentiner, Edwin Gill, Clarence Poe, Justus Bier, Thomas White, and Gordon Hanes to the present array of Museum leaders, too numerous to name here but equally as impressive in their commitment to the Museum's future, North Carolina is the beneficiary of great examples of dedicated leadership.

I am pleased to be chairman of the board of trustees on the occasion of the Museum's Fiftieth Anniversary. It provides an occasion for us to honor the great personalities and moments of the past, to be sure. But of perhaps even greater importance, the anniversary serves as a platform from which to chart a course that enables present and future leaders to nurture a distinguished institution to even greater national distinction.

— CHAIRMAN TERRY SANFORD

Telling the life story of one of North Carolina's — and America's — most distinguished cultural institutions is an occasion to revisit old friends and to enjoy tales oft told and some never told before. The history of the North Carolina Museum of Art includes colorful and prominent personalities, intrigue, controversy, but most important, many of North Carolina's proudest moments over the last fifty years. I hope you will gain pleasure and knowledge from this detailed portrait of your Museum of Art. And from history, may you derive inspiration to help assure the continued vitality and growth of this exceptional cultural asset.

Let us now celebrate as a people the treasures of humanity which are in our public trust and which bring countless pleasures into our lives.

— SECRETARY BETTY RAY McCAIN

The founding of the North Carolina Museum of Art by the General Assembly on April 5, 1947 was one of the boldest and noblest acts by a public body on behalf of the arts in American history. By a narrow margin in the waning hours of the last day of the session, the elected representatives of the people appropriated $1 million to begin a collection of old master and American paintings for the people of the state. When these extraordinary early acquisitions were joined by European paintings and sculptures from the Samuel H. Kress collection, a museum of national importance appeared — almost suddenly — on the horizon, creating quite a stir in the international arts world.

Over the next pages are spread carefully researched insights into the fascinating personalities and strong leaders who have guided the development of this public trust into one of the most significant art museums in the South. I trust you will find great delight and enlightenment in this intriguing story of determined leadership, brilliantly blending public trust, political craftsmanship, and unparalleled opportunity.

— DIRECTOR LAWRENCE J. WHEELER

ACKNOWLEDGEMENTS

This history publication celebrating the first fifty years of the North Carolina Museum of Art recognizes the North Carolina Art Society, the North Carolina State Legislature, the Samuel H. Kress Foundation, and those individuals and groups who helped create the Museum. It recognizes as well those who have supported the growth and development of the Museum since its inception, and it describes the primary goals and visions of its leaders during these five decades.

In addition, the publication includes a chronology recounting as many events and highlights as space and time permit. It includes reminiscences of former and current members of the Museum board of trustees, the boards of the Art Society and NCMA Foundation, as well as former directors and staff—those who have helped shape the Museum's history.

Many people helped with the creation of this publication and I wish to acknowledge them. The support of Lawrence J. Wheeler, director, and Heyward H. McKinney, associate director, the Museum trustees, and the staff has provided both incentive and encouragement. Thanks are due, especially, to Viki Balkcum, Museum publications editor, and Deborah Littlejohn, head graphic designer, for their expertise and invaluable assistance. Also helping to locate and document photographs and providing research assistance were William Holloman, Museum photography services assistant, and Patricia Stack, library assistant. I also wish to thank Bill Gage,

Museum photographer, for his effort to accommodate many requests for his assistance, and Leslie H. Thornbury, television producer-director for the Department of Cultural Resources, who generously shared information he had gathered for a Museum video. Carrie Hedrick, registrar; Marcia Erickson, assistant registrar; Michael Klauke, Museum cataloguer; Peggy D. Jones, business and personnel officer; Dale Pixley, secretary to the director, and her assistant, Becky Booker; Karel R. Shultz, secretary to the associate director; and Theda Tiffany, NCMA Foundation business manager, provided valuable administrative support for the project.

Others who have contributed generously to this publication include Zöe Webster, former executive secretary of the North Carolina Art Society; Beth Paschal, Ann Turner, and Anne Boyer, former presidents of the Art Society; Virginia Camp Smith, loyal patron and supporter of the Museum; Joyce Correll, former coordinator of tours and docents; John Coffey, curator of American and modern art and chair of the curatorial department ; and David Steel, curator of European art — all reviewed the draft of the chronology. George Stevenson, private manuscript archivist for the North Carolina State Archives and his colleagues, Mary Hollis Barnes, archivist, and Steve Massengill, photo archivist, rendered valuable research assistance.

I am particularly grateful to those who have shared some of

their thoughts and memories of the Museum: James B. Byrnes, Ivie L. Clayton, Egbert L. Davis, Jr., Mazie Froelich, Gay M. Hertzman, Thomas S. Kenan III, Dr. Abram Kanof, Beth C. Paschal, Marilyn Perry, Terry Sanford, Mary Semans, Joseph C. Sloane, Rollie Tillman, Ann Turner, and Benjamin F. Williams.

The Museum is especially indebted to Burlington Industries, the Mary Duke Biddle Foundation, Frank J. Turner, Suzanne Reeves McKinney, and the North Carolina Museum of Art Foundation for their support of this publication.

— PEGGY JO D. KIRBY

Peggy Jo D. Kirby, former Museum registrar, retired in 1995 after thirty years at the NCMA. She began her career in 1956 as secretary to the first director, Dr. William R. Valentiner. She became Museum registrar in 1958. In 1963, Kirby and her husband moved to Europe, where she studied art history at universities in Frankfurt, Tübingen and Paris. She returned to the Museum in 1971 as registrar, a position she held until her retirement. Kirby worked under the leadership of all eight Museum directors.

AFTERWORD

Although this publication does not name all those individuals, groups, businesses, and foundations that have supported and worked to develop the Museum during these fifty years, I would especially like to acknowledge the significant contribution of the Museum staff—a contribution that has been and will continue to be an essential part of the Museum's development.

In the words of the late Gordon Hanes at the opening of the new museum building in 1983, in reflecting on what is necessary to create a first-class museum for North Carolina: "Excellence is a curiously powerful and ambiguous word, but we are committed to it in everything we undertake at the North Carolina Museum of Art."

Perhaps this is a commitment upon which we all should reflect when considering our mandate for the next fifty years.

PJDK

The principal sources used in the preparation of this chronology are the Museum's publications and annual reports, including Edgar Peters Bowron, ed., "The North Carolina Museum of Art and its Collections," *Introduction to the Collections, North Carolina Museum of Art* (Raleigh, 1983, revised edition 1992); and *The North Carolina Museum of Art: A Brief History* (Raleigh, 1986). Also referenced were minutes from meetings of the NCMA Board of Trustees and the Art Society Board of Directors. Other sources include *North Carolina Architect, Special Issue: 20th Anniversary North Carolina Museum of Art 1947–1967*, Vol. 4 & 5, May–June (Raleigh, 1967); Ola Maie Foushee, *Art in North Carolina: Episodes and Developments, 1585–1970* (Chapel Hill, 1972); *The North Carolina Art Society, 1976 Annual Report, 50th Anniversary* (Raleigh, 1976); Margaret Sterne, *The Passionate Eye: The Life of William R. Valentiner* (Detroit, 1980); and *Guide to Research Materials in the North Carolina State Archives: State Agency Records* (Raleigh, 1995).

Paragraphs in italic type refer to art activities and events in North Carolina; however they do not relate directly to the North Carolina Museum of Art.

A SELECTED CHRONOLOGY

TO MAKE ART THE PROPERTY OF ALL, 1903 – 1946

> "The North Carolina State Art Society . . . made an immediate cultural impact that has endured for a half century . . . . Its history is inextricably interwoven with the history of the North Carolina Museum of Art."
>
> —*Ola Maie Foushee*, *Art in North Carolina*

1. John J. Blair (far left), first president of the Fine Arts Society (1924 – 1926), and Katherine Pendleton Arrington (president, 1926 – 1955) meet with representatives of the Grand Central Galleries, New York, at the Sir Walter Hotel, Raleigh, in 1926. Reprinted by permission of the NC Division of Archives and History and *The News & Observer* of Raleigh, North Carolina.

1903 Still struggling from Civil War losses and the upheavals of Reconstruction, North Carolina nevertheless begins to assert its cultural consciousness by acquiring portraits, monuments, and sculptures to honor its heroes.

The General Assembly creates the North Carolina Historical Commission, and its members, along with other interested people, begin working to stimulate public interest in the idea of a state art museum.[1]

1912 The North Carolina Literary and Historical Association organizes.

1915 Clarence H. Poe, young editor of the *Progressive Farmer* magazine and an outspoken advocate of art education for children, suggests establishing a state art commission and encourages that reproductions of famous paintings related to rural life be placed in public schools.

1.

1924 Twelve members of the State Literary and Historical Association, interested in forming a fine arts society, hold their first meeting. Mary Lee McMillan encouraged Robert Burton House, secretary of the association, and John J. Blair, head of Schoolhouse Planning, to call the meeting. Others present include Mamie Elliot London, Katherine Pendleton Arrington, Mary Lee McMillan, and Clarence H. Poe. The members organize the Fine Arts Society as a branch of the Literary and Historical Association.

The first action of the society is to endorse the creation of an art collection and museum for the people of North Carolina.

1925 In December, the Fine Arts Society holds its first annual meeting. An exhibition of paintings, primarily from the Grand Central Galleries in New York, is shown in the parlors of the old Meredith College on Blount Street in Raleigh. The society's first speaker is Homer Saint-Gaudens, director of the Carnegie Institute of Fine Arts in Pittsburgh.

Thus, the Fine Arts Society establishes a pattern in which well-known speakers and exhibitions become part of its annual meetings. The tradition becomes an important part of the society's contribution to the state's cultural life.

1926 The Fine Arts Society, now separated from the State Literary and Historical Association, meets and elects Katherine Pendleton Arrington president. The primary goal endorsed at the meeting is to generate interest in creating a state art museum in Raleigh.

1.

1.   William Merritt Chase, *The Artist's Daughter, Alice*, was given to the N. C. Art Society as part of the Robert F. Phifer collection in 1928.

2.   Art Society's first exhibition gallery, provided by the state in 1929.

3.   Robert F. Phifer, the major donor in the early history of the Art Society.

2.

1927 The Fine Arts Society receives its charter of incorporation on October 7, under the name The North Carolina State Art Society. Arrington donates the society's first work of art, *Mammy*, by the American painter Gari Melchers.

Upon learning of the new Art Society, North Carolina native Robert Fullenwider Phifer, a wealthy businessman who has resided for many years in New York, writes John Blair of his desire to leave his collection to a gallery in his native state. Blair promises that the Art Society will find a suitable place, and in December, Phifer bequeaths his collection of paintings and funds, held in trust, to the society.[2]

1928 Phifer dies on October 16. The Robert F. Phifer Bequest funds, administered by the Art Society, are subject to a restriction: only works of art may be purchased with the interest accrued from the fund. The bequest cannot be used to cover salaries or other expenses. (By 1997, the North Carolina Museum of Art purchases more than two hundred fifty works for its collection with funds from the Phifer Bequest.)

1929 The Art Society requests that the North Carolina General Assembly place it under state patronage and control. Although the ensuing legislation fails to appropriate any funds to the organization, it does authorize the state to provide exhibition space for works of art owned or on loan to the society. A temporary "art museum" (in reality, only an exhibition gallery in the state agriculture building) opens on February 26, with an exhibition of paintings from the Phifer Bequest and other works that the Art Society received during its first five years.

The bill passed by the General Assembly also stipulates that "the governing body of the North Carolina State Art Society, Inc. shall be a board of directors con

3.

"As a result of the Phifer Bequest,
the Art Society became the beneficiary
and manager of an endowment
that grew to over $4 million in
the 1980s."
— Rollie Tillman, Art Society
President, 1994–present

sisting of sixteen members of whom the governor of the state, the Superintendent of Public Instruction, the Attorney General, and the chairman of the art committee of the North Carolina Federation of Women's Clubs shall be ex-officio members, and four others shall be named by the governor of the state. The remaining eight directors shall be chosen by the members of the North Carolina State Art Society in such a manner and terms as that body shall determine."[3]

1931 *The North Carolina Association of Professional Artists is the first statewide group of "professional" artists formed for the purpose of helping members sell their work.[4] Among the group's charter members are Elliott Daingerfield, Blowing Rock; Henry Jay MacMillan, Wilmington; Mabel Pugh, Raleigh; and Francis Speight, Philadelphia. In April, the newly formed group holds its first exhibition in Hill Hall at the University of North Carolina. Subsequently, the State Art Society asks the group to exhibit its work at the society's annual meeting in Raleigh in December 1932.[5]*

1933 *The State of North Carolina issues a certificate of incorporation to Black Mountain College. Ultimately, the arts assume the central role in the school's curriculum, and Josef Albers becomes head of the art department (1933 – 1949). Subsequently, in 1950, Albers joins the newly formed Department of Design at the School of Fine Arts, Yale University. He remains at Yale until his retirement in 1958.*

1. A graphic invitation, about 1939.

2. A poster displays statistics of the WPA Art Center in Raleigh.

3. The state granted permission for the Art Society to occupy a space on the second floor of the former Supreme Court Building, Raleigh, in 1939.

3.

1.

2.

1935 The federal Works Projects Administration (WPA) chooses North Carolina as the site of the national headquarters for the Federal Art Project (FAP), a branch of the WPA, and Raleigh becomes the first city in the nation to have a federally supported art center. Later, the center in Raleigh becomes the model for other federally supported centers in North Carolina and the nation. Typically, each center consists of three principal parts: gallery, school, and extension activities. Eventually there are nine centers in North Carolina: Raleigh, Winston-Salem, Asheville, Concord, Greensboro, Sanford, Greenville, Kinston, and Wilmington.

By December 1938, only three years after the inception of the FAP, more than four million people have attended art centers in North Carolina. The program's national director, Holger Cahill, said as he traveled the state, ". . . the WPA-FAP project does more than provide a livelihood for artists, the program tends to make art the property of all rather than the hobby of a few."[6]

1936 The dedication of the first art museum in North Carolina occurs in Charlotte in a building that was a branch of the former United States Mint and is now known as the Mint Museum of Art.

4.

5.

6.

7.

4.   Painting class for high school students at a WPA Extension Art Center, 1940.

5.   Children's drawing class, WPA, 1940.

6.   WPA-sponsored class for adults, 1940.

7.   School children view an exhibition at the Crosby-Garfield WPA Extension Gallery in 1940.

All photographs these pages courtesy of WPA Federal Art Project.

1937 *The Association of Professional Artists sponsors the state's first juried exhibition, in the new Person Hall Art Gallery at the University of North Carolina. The jury members select 42 of the 132 works submitted, representing the work of 39 artists including Isabelle Bowen Henderson, Henry Jay MacMillan, and a non-member, Claude Howell. The show is the genesis for what later becomes the* North Carolina Artists Exhibition.

The Association of Professional Artists appears to have ceased activity after 1937.

1939 After the Art Society makes numerous requests for additional space, the state grants it permission to occupy an area on the second floor of the former Supreme Court Building in Raleigh. The new Art Society Gallery officially opens in March with an exhibition of American paintings selected from several galleries in New York City. Artists represented include Winslow Homer, John Singer Sargent, Thomas Eakins, Gari Melchers, and Mary Cassatt.[7]

In October, the Art Society board of directors approves the society's affiliation with the Raleigh Federal Arts Project Center. The FAP agrees to provide a staff to operate the society's gallery, publicize exhibitions, and promote statewide art

activities. The exhibition program is sponsored jointly by the FAP and the Art Society and supervised by an Art Society committee.[8]

The annual meeting of the Art Society in December continues the tradition of featuring a well-known speaker and a special exhibition, usually from a gallery in New York. The Museum of Modern Art, New York, lends twenty-five watercolors for the occasion. The principal speaker is Alfred M. Frankfurter, editor of *Art News* magazine and a member of the 1939 World's Fair committee for the *Masterpieces of Art* exhibition.

Four artists represent North Carolina at the 1939 World's Fair, through the auspices of the Federal Art Project. Selected

1.

through several screening processes are Claude Howell and Henry J. MacMillan, Wilmington; Richard Lofton, Winston-Salem; and Nathan Ornoff, Durham.[9]

The director of the Detroit Institute of Arts, William R. Valentiner (later the North Carolina Museum of Art's first director), is director-general of the exhibition *Masterpieces of Art*.

1940 – 1942 *Robert Lee Humber, a native of Greenville, North Carolina, who lived and worked in Paris as an international lawyer for several years, returns to Greenville and launches an international movement for a world federation: an organization allowing each country to retain domestic sovereignty, delegating to a world government only those powers needed to maintain law and order. In late 1940 and early 1941, he travels throughout North Carolina promoting this movement. His efforts are rewarded when, in March 1941, North Carolina becomes the first state to endorse the concept of a world federation. In 1945, Humber represents the Southern Council on International Relations at the conference in San Francisco that for-* *mulates the charter of the United Nations. Humber continues his crusade in other states as well. By March 1950, the legislatures of sixteen states have endorsed the movement.[10]*

2.

1.　　　A Depression-era photo of downtown Raleigh.

2.　　　Katherine Pendleton Arrington (second from left) at a 1940 exhibition opening in the State Art Gallery. Photo: WPA Federal Art Project.

1943 In March, after almost four years of continuous affiliation between the Art Society and the Federal Art Project Center, the FAP Center in Raleigh closes. (The Works Projects Administration and the FAP end all project support throughout the United States on April 30, 1943.)

After federal support ends, the State Art Society once again asks the North Carolina General Assembly for assistance, and also changes the name of its gallery to State Art Gallery. With the support of Governor John Melville Broughton (1941–45), the Art Society persuades the General Assembly to appropriate funds to support the arts. The bill appropriates a grant-in-aid of $2,000 annually for the 1943–45 biennium, providing funds for gallery

office space, lighting, heating, and a director's salary. The society assumes all other expenses. (The North Carolina Symphony also receives, for the first time, a state appropriation. The General Assembly passes the so-called "horn-tootin" bill, Senate Bill 248, 1943.)[11]

In June, Governor Broughton further aids the society's efforts to construct a new gallery by appointing a Citizen's Committee for a State Art Gallery. Committee members include former Governor J.C.B. Ehringhaus, The Honorable Josephus Daniels, Clarence H. Poe, Katherine Pendleton Arrington, R. D. W. Conner, Robert B. House, and Chairman Robert Lee Humber. The committee makes an unsuccessful effort to accumulate $50,000 to construct

a suitable building. Perhaps to gain popular support for the idea, some members suggest that the new art gallery also serve as a memorial to the state's veterans from the two world wars.

In October, the Art Society sponsors an exhibition of the work of Anni and Josef Albers at the State Art Gallery. *The Two-Albers Show* includes twenty-two paintings and eighteen prints by Josef Albers and eighteen hand-woven textiles by Anni Albers.

1.

2.

1. North Carolina artist Claude Howell's work on display in the State Art Gallery, 1944.

2. Lena B. Davis with her exhibition at the State Art Gallery in 1951. Reprinted by permission of the NC Division of Archives and History and *The News & Observer* of Raleigh, North Carolina.

3. Augusta Rembert speaks about her work with students at the State Art Gallery in 1945. Photo from *Raleigh Times*, May 14, 1945.

4. A 1948 meeting of the Art Society with Robert L. Humber (first on left), Clarence Poe (fifth from left), Mamie Elliot London (seventh from left), and Katherine Pendleton Arrington (fourth from right). Reprinted by permission of the NC Division of Archives and History and *The News & Observer* of Raleigh, North Carolina.

3.

1944 The State Art Gallery hosts its first one-man exhibition, featuring the work of artist Claude Howell.

The featured speaker for the annual meeting of the Art Society in December is Rensselaer W. Lee, editor of *Art Bulletin* and executive secretary of the American Council of Learned Societies for the Protection of Cultural Treasures in the War Area.

North Carolina gains its second permanent art museum with the dedication of the Hickory Museum of Art on February 4. The Honorable Clyde R. Hoey, former governor and senator, is speaker for the occasion.[12]

1945 The North Carolina General Assembly passes a joint resolution authorizing Governor Broughton to appoint a special commission, composed of five citizens, to study a building program for the state and determine space requirements for "constitutional" offices. The bill specifically mentions a building for the State Art Gallery.[13]

1946 As a feature for its twentieth anniversary year, the State Art Society sponsors the first juried competition offering sizable monetary awards for North Carolina artists. Mamie London, the gallery director and a founding member of the society, is largely responsible for raising funds for the awards totaling $1,000. The society also sponsors the exhibition *School of Paris*, consisting of the work of fourteen artists, including Juan Gris and Max Ernst.

THE BIRTH OF THE NORTH CAROLINA MUSEUM OF ART, 1947–1955

"In the 175 years of our history, this State
never has been able to establish a great art gallery;
but it is now within our grasp."
—*Governor Kerr Scott*

1947 "Art has been and is the barometer of human progress," Robert Lee Humber tells the Sir Walter Cabinet, an influential and prestigious organization of wives of state legislators.[14] In the three years since Governor J. Melville Broughton appointed him chairman of the Citizen's Committee for a State Art Gallery, he has received unanimous support from North Carolinians for establishing a state art museum of old master paintings, Humber says.

In 1943, Humber carried his crusade to New York City, where he eventually was introduced to Samuel H. Kress and began a four-year negotiation with the noted philanthropist. In 1947, Humber obtains a verbal commitment from Kress to contribute $1 million to help establish a state

art museum, with two conditions. First, the donor is to remain anonymous and the offer remain verbal. Second, other sources must match the proposed gift. Humber accepts Kress's challenge and asks the North Carolina legislature to appropriate $1 million to match the offer. During his fight to ensure passage of this milestone legislation, Humber obtains the support of Governor Robert Gregg Cherry (1945–49); Brandon Hodges, the governor's legislative advisor; Senator Joseph Blythe; and Representative John H. Kerr, Jr.[15]

Representative Kerr introduces the legislation to the State House of Representatives by saying: "Mr. Speaker, I know that I am facing a hostile audience, but

man cannot live by bread alone." Kerr's eloquent speech is followed with considerable debate and parliamentary maneuvering, but finally, by a narrow margin, House Bill 862 is passed.[16]

In the state senate, Bill 395 is introduced by Senator Joseph Blythe and subsequently becomes law.[17]

The legislation earmarks $1 million to the North Carolina State Art Society, "which appropriation shall not be made available for expenditure ... until the sum of one million dollars shall have been secured through gifts and paid into the State Treasury ...." The bill also stipulates that after allocating all other appropriations at the end of the 1947–49 biennium, there must be a surplus in the state

"It was about the same time John Kerr and others were discussing the $1 million appropriation that I first became associated with the State Art Gallery. I came to Raleigh from Chapel Hill, where I was studying, in order to volunteer at the gallery. I did a variety of things at the gallery — from driving nails to sweeping floors, to mailing brochures. I was willing to do anything and I thought it all very fascinating. My first year of working with the North Carolina Artists Competition in 1946 was probably the most interesting experience I had ever known."
— Benjamin F. Williams, Curator, 1956–79

1.

26–27

general fund of at least $1 million. Many legislators support the bill only because they doubt that these two conditions will ever be met. [18]

Newspapers issue editorials both for and against the new legislation. *The High Point Enterprise* calls the appropriation "foolish" and advocates spending the money for education instead. *The Greensboro Daily News* retorts that "we haven't heard that the teachers have raised any kick against the proposed art gallery, and that may be because they consider art and education to be closely linked . . . . There is no competition among lighthouses." [19]

The legislature increases the State Art Society's annual appropriation from $2,000 to $5,000. (By 1949, the grant has been increased to $6,000 annually, and in 1951, to $10,000.) With the increase, the society is able to employ its first gallery assistant, Lucy Cherry Crisp. In September, Crisp becomes gallery director and eventually executive secretary of the State Art Society. She immediately begins a monthly publication, *North Carolina News of Art*, which she edits until her retirement in 1955.

1949 *Winston-Salem, North Carolina becomes the second city in the United States to form an arts council. Soon afterwards, Corpus Christi, Texas, the first city to form an arts council, dissolves it, giving Winston-Salem the distinction of having founded the oldest city arts council in the country.* [20]

Wake Forest College (now Wake Forest University) awards Robert Lee Humber a LL.D. degree.

1.

2.

1951 Humber continues his efforts to persuade the Kress Foundation to honor the verbal commitment Samuel H. Kress made to him in 1947. Shortly after making the promise, Kress's health failed and his brother, Rush H. Kress, assumed management of the foundation. Finally, in January 1951, Kress assures Humber that the foundation will cooperate with him in his efforts to "enlist the financial support of the people of North Carolina, its outstanding citizens and families ... so that they will take a deep, personal, active interest in the proper organization and administration of the State Museum of Art of North Carolina to make it an inspiration and center of art education." The foundation promises to include Raleigh in

its program to establish galleries throughout the United States that will receive a Kress collection of paintings "consisting of outstanding Italian Renaissance Art and other similar paintings of a value of at least one million dollars."[21]

Kress's offer of paintings instead of funds presents a legislative obstacle. The Act of 1947 obligated the state to match "donations" of $1 million, and debate arises about whether the Kress offer of paintings of an equal value complies with those terms. Governor William Kerr Scott (1949 – 1953), Lieutenant Governor H. P. Taylor, House Speaker W. Frank Taylor, and Representative William B. Rodman of Beaufort are among those who support acceptance of the Kress offer, believing it

meets the spirit of the terms of the 1947 act.

The issue sparks considerable debate and controversy, both in and out of the state legislature. Some legislators want to repeal the 1947 "contingency" appropriation act and return the money to the state general fund. As early as 1949, Representative Fred Royster had introduced a bill in the house to repeal the act.

However, the General Assembly passes House Bill 1086 in April 1951, permitting the North Carolina State Art Society to accept a gift of paintings from the Kress Foundation. The bill also specifies that the $1 million appropriated by the state in the Act of 1947 will match the gift of paintings from Kress and be used for the pur

–3.   Gallery views from the *Design for Today* exhibition at the State Art Gallery in October 1950.

hase of works of art.

"In our measured judgment," reads a joint message from the governor, the speaker of the house, and the lieutenant governor, "We cannot afford to reject the Kress offer. In the 175 years of our history, the State never has been able to establish a great art gallery; but it is now within our grasp. Any state of this Union would not only welcome such an opportunity, but would exert itself zealously to obtain it. Surely, it would be unwise for us now to fumble the ball."[22]

Governor Scott appoints five members of the State Art Society to a State Art Commission (the formation of a commission is a provision of the Act of 1947), which will have sole authority to use the appropriated funds to purchase art. Members of the commission are Robert Lee Humber, Chairman; Katherine Pendleton Arrington;[23] Edwin M. Gill;[24] Clarence H. Poe;[25] and Clemens Sommer.[26]

The State Art Commission names Carl W. Hamilton of New York its unofficial advisor. Hamilton, who served without pay until 1954, is a well-known art dealer and collector of Italian Renaissance paintings. (It was he who had earlier introduced Humber to Stephen S. Pichetto, then the curator of the Kress Collection.[27]) In September, the State Art Gallery, under joint support of the North Carolina State Art Society and the State of North Carolina, moves into a new and larger facility. The state provides quarters in the new wing of the Education Building in Raleigh. (The gallery remains at that location until January 1955.)

Volunteers from the Junior League of Raleigh begin assisting at the State Art Gallery. One early volunteer, Mrs. Charles Lee Smith, Jr., later serves as chairman of the Art Society's hospitality and tour committees and remains a loyal volunteer and donor to the NCMA.

The opening exhibition at the new gallery, *Glass of Yesterday and Today*, includes a collection of more than sixty pieces of Greek and Roman glass donated to the Art Society. (George Pratt of New York gave the collection to Katherine Pendleton Arrington, who in turn gave it to the Art Society shortly after its found-

1. 2. 3.

1 – 3   Ancient glass from the Pratt collection included in the *Glass of Yesterday and Today* exhibition.

ing in 1926. The Art Society transferred the collection to the NCMA in 1961.) The modern glass shown in the exhibition is from the Leerdam Glassworks in Holland.

The North Carolina State Art Society celebrates its twenty-fifth anniversary in December with an exhibition entitled *Paintings from Three Centuries*, lent by Knoedler Galleries of New York. The exhibition includes nineteen paintings dating from the eighteenth to the twentieth century by Ruisdael, Copley, Cézanne, Monet, Homer, and Picasso.

1952 An amendment added to the Act of 1951 creates a problem for both the Art Society and the State Art Commission. Prior to the purchase of works of art, the amendment requires the commission to obtain the approval of the Art Society board of directors and either the director or the chief curator of the National Gallery of Art in Washington. In January 1952, the National Gallery board refuses to accept this responsibility, making any purchases impossible under the current law.

The Art Society and the Art Commission propose to the NC attorney general that William R. Valentiner be considered as the approving authority. Internationally recognized, Valentiner is an eminent scholar and art historian in the fields of

Italian Renaissance sculpture, Dutch seventeenth-century painting, and German expressionist art. Valentiner was director of the Detroit Institute of Arts from 1924 to 1945. He was co-director of the Los Angeles County Museum from 1946 to 1949 and continues to serve as a consultant there. Later, in 1954, Valentiner becomes founding director of the J. Paul Getty Museum until he resigns in 1955.

The Art Commission had already selected many works, which were being held in New York until December 31, 1951. With less than a month left before the purchase deadline, Valentiner appraises 180 paintings, and Humber presents the findings to the attorney general, who agrees to name Valentiner as the substi-

"The dealers in New York were eager to sell paintings at that time [1947 – 51], a time in which the market was rich with good paintings, many formerly in British collections, sold to pay debts after the war. Because the British had collected Dutch and Flemish masters, the New York art market was particularly well supplied with examples of paintings from these two areas."
— *Benjamin F. Williams*

"The advisor recommended to make the decisions about which paintings to choose for this milepost collection was William R. Valentiner. Known to the European and American art world as the authority on Rembrandt, he had helped build the collections of four major museums, and had published more books, catalogues and articles than could be counted."
— *Beth Cummings Paschal, Museum Trustee Emeritus*

tute approving authority. Humber telephones the galleries and tells them to expect payment right after the New Year's holiday. Then the attorney general wavers on his decision, and the case is ultimately sent to the State Supreme Court. Valentiner's appointment is upheld and the legal issues are resolved by February 1952.[28]

The lack of an approving authority delayed the purchase of the first group of works chosen by the Art Commission. However, in April the commission, with the concurrence of Valentiner, submits an initial list of 147 paintings to the Art Society board of directors for final approval. The value of the paintings recommended for purchase is $809,000.[29]

The Art Society formally adopts the name "North Carolina Museum of Art" to replace "State Art Gallery."[30]

1953 – 1955 Working from the initial listing of 147 approved paintings, the Art Commission purchases a total of 157 paintings with funds from the state appropriation.[31] The commission also acquires twenty-four paintings with funds from the Phifer Bequest,[32] and purchases twenty-one paintings, using a combination of state appropriations and Phifer Bequest funds.[33] In 1953, the North Carolina General Assembly enacts legislation that permits the State Art Society to exchange paintings "for other works of art, which, in the opinion of the State Art Society board of directors, would improve the quality, value or representative character of its art collection."[34] The commission acquires twenty-six works which

1.

2.

*"Accustomed to working with volun-
teers, [Byrnes] made a timely appeal
to the Junior League of Raleigh and
they responded with a team of twelve
seasoned helpers . . . . They under-
went on-the-job training in
cataloguing books, filing, labeling,
pasting, typing, collating, speaking.
At this point, it would not be an
extreme exaggeration to describe the
understaffed and underbudgeted
Museum as a cottage industry."*
— Beth Cummings Paschal

include Gothic and Renaissance furniture, sculpture, and decorative arts, through trades and exchanges. With the support of Governor William B. Umstead (1953–54), the General Assembly appropriates $200,000 for renovating and converting the former State Highway Building on East Morgan Street in Raleigh into an art museum.

In September 1953, the state names a Raleigh architect, Edwin Waugh, responsible for overseeing the renovation and conversion of the building. The State Art Society board of directors appoints Henry L. Kamphoefner, dean of the North Carolina State College School of Design; Carl W. Hamilton, advisor to the Art Commission; and Noah W. Sites, Jr., representing the

State Budget Bureau, as consultants to the building committee. Serving on the committee are Chairman Robert Lee Humber, Clarence Poe, Clemens Sommer, Isabelle Bowen Henderson, Sylvester Green, and Edwin Gill.

The Art Society board of directors retains Carl W. Hamilton as an art consultant and advisor to the North Carolina Museum of Art and the North Carolina State Art Society.35

Renovation of the former Highway Building begins in August 1954. At the end of December 1955, at a cost of $400,000 (twice the original appropriation), the building is ready to receive works of art. Some works purchased by the Art Commission have been stored in warehouses

in New York — in some instances, for more than three years.

The Museum appoints Valentiner as its first director. He rapidly appoints key members of his staff: James B. Byrnes, associate director; Benjamin F. Williams, curator of exhibitions; and May Davis Hill, curator of prints, librarian, and registrar.

Byrnes had worked seven years with Valentiner at the Los Angeles County Museum and, most recently, served as director of the Colorado Springs Fine Arts Center. Byrnes studied at the National Academy of Design and the Art Students League in New York, Columbia University, New York University, and the University of Perugia, in Italy.

Williams had been assistant to the

*"In the summer of 1955, I received
a letter from Dr. Valentiner saying
that he was returning from Italy
sooner than expected because 'Like
Cincinnatus of old, I am again called
from retirement, this time to become
director of the Raleigh Museum.' "*
—James B. Byrnes

The State Highway
Building during its conversion to an art
museum, 1954.

North Carolina state offi-
cials visit the State Highway Building
during renovation. In the center is
Governor Luther Hodges, with Edwin Gill
(second from right).

Paintings begin arriving at
the new museum in 1955. Pictured (left
to right) are two unidentified art
handlers, Ben Williams, James Byrnes,
and Director Valentiner.

3.

Director of the State Art Gallery since
1949. A graduate of the University of
North Carolina at Chapel Hill, Williams
also studied at Columbia University Extension in Paris.

May Davis Hill earned degrees in art
history and library science at the University of North Carolina at Chapel Hill. She
was formerly on the staff of the Cooper
Union Museum in New York, as assistant
to the keeper of drawings and prints, and
staff lecturer at the Metropolitan Museum of Art. Prior to her appointment at the
museum, she was a general college librarian at UNC at Chapel Hill.

In December 1955, the State Art Society elects Robert Lee Humber president,
succeeding Katherine Arrington, who died
in April, after serving nearly thirty years.
Humber, then vice-president of the society, had been serving as presiding officer
after Arrington became ill in 1952. The Art
Society elects Edwin M. Gill vice-president.

1.   Paintings arrive at the new
Museum for the *Valentiner Memorial
Exhibition* in 1959.

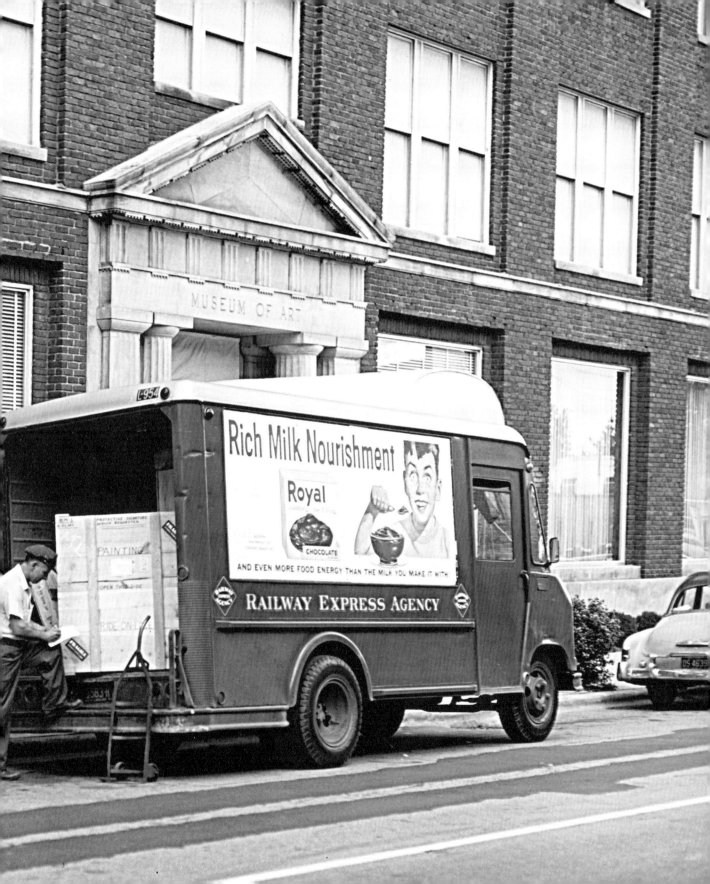

THE MIRACLE ON MORGAN STREET, 1956–1960

"The Museum opened in the grandest style possible, April 6, 1956. Streets were closed to allow assembling; National Guard personnel were in place in uniform; waiting to enter were members of the press, national and international, and elegant visitors by the hundreds."

—*Beth Cummings Paschal*

1956 The North Carolina Museum of Art opens on April 6, 1956. At the opening Robert Lee Humber states: "The birth of this institution is a sovereign confirmation of the conviction that faith is still the most potent force on earth."[36] Governor Hodges calls the museum "a logical outgrowth of a mental attitude regarding education which had dominated North Carolinians since 1900 . . . embracing not only things that are useful and practical, but also those intangibles that nurture the soul of man."[37]

Time magazine describes the endeavor as "the newest major art museum in the United States and the first to have a collection subsidized by state funds."[38]

In his introduction to *The Catalogue of Paintings*, Valentiner writes: "The creation of the North Carolina Museum of Art is a unique achievement, not only in the history of American museums, but in that of the whole museum world. As far as we know, this is the first time that so large a sum has been appropriated by a government body for the acquisition of a public collection of paintings prior to the construction of a new building to house them. This was an exceedingly wise move on the part of the State; no doubt other states and cities will follow North Carolina's example in the future."[39]

Art News, *Time*, and *Life* magazines publish articles including color reproductions of the paintings in the collection.

Within its first year of operation, Valentiner proposes expanding the permanent collection to include sculpture, decorative arts, and modern art. He donates a sizeable painting by Richard Diebenkorn, *Berkeley No. 8*. To encourage other donations and to stimulate purchases of contemporary and modern art, the director gives the Museum several modern paintings.[40]

The first major loan exhibition, *French Painting of the Second Half of the Nineteenth Century*, takes place in June 1956. Artists represented include Corot, Gauguin, Manet, Monet, Renoir, and Van Gogh. The paintings are on loan from the Museum of Fine Arts, Boston; the Baltimore Museum of Art; as well as from private collectors and dealers in New York.

Governor Luther Hodges cuts the ribbon at Museum opening ceremonies on Morgan Street.

. Forward-looking citizens: Robert Lee Humber (left) and Carl Hamilton at the 1956 opening.

. The lobby of the former Highway Building, now a museum.

. Robert Lee Humber (front left) sees his efforts pay off at the long-awaited opening ceremonies.

All photos this page reprinted by permission of the NC Division of Archives and History and *The News & Observer* of Raleigh, North Carolina.

In December, the nineteenth *North Carolina Artists Exhibition* opens. This now-annual event evolved from the 1937 Association of Professional Artists juried exhibition and is sponsored by the Art Society.

The director endorses the first loans from the new collection to other museums. The Milwaukee Art Institute requests the loan of the Museum's painting *Still Life with Game* by Luis Meléndez for the exhibition, *Still Life*, that opens at the Art Institute in September 1956 and afterwards travels to the Cincinnati Art Museum.

Valentiner plans an exhibition to commemorate the three-hundred-fiftieth anniversary of the birth of Rembrandt. It is the only exhibition of its kind in the United States (there are seven commemorative exhibitions in Europe). To help finance the project, the Museum charges each adult visitor fifty cents for admission. The *Art News* annual edition selects *Rembrandt and His Pupils* as one of the four best exhibitions in the nation in 1956 – 57.

The Museum's collection continues to grow during its first years. Through the distinguished reputation of Valentiner and the continuing efforts of Humber, the Museum receives several paintings as gifts, including *Adoration of the Shepherds* by Jacob Jordaens, a gift of John Motley Morehead. The Humbers donate *Madonna and Child*, by the Italian artist Guido Reni. The family of Dr. Charles Lee Smith, whose son, Charles Lee Smith, Jr., was treasurer of the State Art Society for seventeen years, donates to the American collection *Porthole Portrait of George Washington*, by Rembrandt Peale. A second-century A.D. Roman marble sculpture, *Herakles*, is a gift from Mr. and Mrs. Jack Linsky of New York. The Museum library receives contributions of books and funds from the North Carolina Federation of Women's Clubs and other book clubs in the state.

Black Mountain College closes September 27, 1956.

"The Museum did indeed open, but not until a small, last minute contretemps had been settled. Word had come to Valentiner and Byrnes that certain ladies in high places had been offended . . . by the nudity of the Roman male figures in the lobby. So it was that Byrnes, whose skills were numberless, spent precious last-minute time modeling and applying quasi-fig leaves to the Romans . . . ."
— Beth Cummings Paschal

1.

1.   Director Valentiner (left) with Museum guests. Reprinted by permission of the NC Division of Archives and History and *The News & Observer* of Raleigh, North Carolina.

2.   Billboards spread news of the 1956 Rembrandt exhibition around the state.

THE NORTH CAROLINA MUSEUM OF ART
PRESENTS A SPECIAL EXHIBITION

RALEIGH, NORTH CAROLINA

Rembrandt AND HIS PUPILS

CELEBRATING THE 350TH ANNIVERSARY OF REMBRANDT'S BIRTH

NOVEMBER 17 THROUGH DECEMBER 31

DONATION FIFTY CENTS

THE MUSEUM'S PERMANENT COLLECTION IS FREE TO THE PUBLIC

CLOSED MONDAY

General Outdoor Adv Co

2.

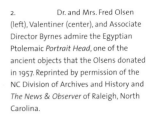

1.

2.

1957 The NCMA receives its first state government biennial appropriation, which includes $10,000 to establish an art purchase fund.

Five new staff positions are added, including a curator of education. The staff now numbers twenty-one (including the guards).

Valentiner and the staff install four new galleries. One contains a collection of Egyptian, Greek, and Roman art, a gift from Dr. and Mrs. Fred Olsen of Guilford, Connecticut. Another gallery contains Renaissance and Baroque sculpture. There is also a print room exhibiting Dutch, Italian, and German prints from the fifteenth to eighteenth century.

The Museum begins publishing the *Bulletin* and *Calendar of Art Events*. It opens an art rental-sales gallery, "to offer for sale original works of art by well-known American and European artists at prices attractive to the young collector."[41]

Valentiner receives the Cross of the Order of Merit from the president of the Federal Republic of Germany and an honorary LL.D. degree from Duke University. He completes his book *Rembrandt and Spinoza: A Study of the Spiritual Conflicts in Seventeenth Century Holland*, published in London by Phaidon Press.

Contributions from private and corporate sources in North Carolina support the director's plan to expand the Museum's collection. Mr. and Mrs. Arthur W. Levy, Jr., donate a bronze *Neptune*, attrib-

uted to Benvenuto Cellini, and two marble angels, by Agostino Cornacchini, for the Italian sculpture collection. Wachovia Bank and Trust Company contribute funds to purchase the earliest painting in the European collection: *Madonna and Child*, from the circle of Italian artist Berlinghiero.

During these early years, the Museum also begins to receive twentieth-century American and European paintings as gifts. One of the earliest and most important of this group, *The Green Bridge II*, by American artist Lyonel Feininger, is a gift of Mrs. Ferdinand Möller in honor of Valentiner. Two other friends of Valentiner donate paintings: *Untitled*, 1934, by the French artist Jean Hélion, from Pegg

3.   Lyonel Feininger, *The Green Bridge II*, a gift of Mrs. Ferdinand Möller in 1957.

4.   Richard Diebenkorn, *Berkeley No. 8*, a gift of W.R. Valentiner.

5.   Director Valentiner (seated) shares observations on German Expressionism during the *Ernst Ludwig Kirchner* exhibition in 1958. Reprinted by permission of the NC Division of Archives and History and *The News & Observer* of Raleigh, North Carolina.

6.   Former U.S. President Harry Truman (center) was among the distinguished guests in the Museum's early years. He is shown here with Robert Lee Humber (left), Governor Hodges (background), and James Byrnes (right of Truman) in 1958.

Guggenheim; and *Blue Landscape*, by the American artist Milton Avery, a gift from Roy Neuberger. James B. Byrnes and his wife, Barbara, give the Museum *Sketch for the Crucifixion*, by American artist Rico Lebrun.

One important donation, approximately 4,200 books and collection catalogues, is a gift to the Museum library from the Levy Galleries of New York.

1958 In January, the NCMA opens the first museum-sponsored exhibition in the United States devoted to the German expressionist painter Ernst Ludwig Kirchner (1880 – 1938). Valentiner organizes the exhibition consisting of ninety-seven oil paintings, watercolors, and prints. He also writes the comprehensive catalogue.

Charles W. Stanford becomes curator of education. A graduate of the University of North Carolina at Chapel Hill, Stanford continued his studies at Teacher's College, Columbia University, and Princeton University Graduate School. Before coming to the NCMA, he was on the staff at Colonial Williamsburg, Virginia.

On September 6, Valentiner dies at the age of seventy-eight in New York,

shortly after returning from Europe. Associate Director Byrnes becomes the acting director.

Edwin M. Gill, state treasurer and vice-president of the State Art Society, writes a resolution regarding his friend Valentiner. Incorporated into the minutes of the annual meeting of the Art Society, the resolution states: "After his death, we learned from his will that Valentiner had left to our Museum a collection of paintings, drawings, and sculptures, as well as his unique library of books relating to the history of art; but nothing that he left us in his will can compare with the priceless heritage of his wisdom, which he made available to us during our formative years while he served as our director. He brought

1.   Acting Director Byrnes
(right) plans the 1959 *Valentiner
Memorial Exhibition* with Paul Wescher,
director of the Getty Museum. Reprinted
by permission of the NC Division of
Archives and History and *The News &
Observer* of Raleigh, North Carolina.

2.   (left to right) Clarence Poe,
Beth Cummings Paschal, and a guest
view Lanino's *Madonna Enthroned with
Saints and Donors* as the Museum pre-
pares for the Kress collection opening.
Reprinted by permission of the NC
Division of Archives and History and *The
News & Observer* of Raleigh, North
Carolina.

to our young institution his experience of
fifty years in the development and administration of art museums. He left us his
poise, his independence of judgment, his
integrity . . . as guides for our future."

Shortly after Valentiner's death, three
prominent North Carolinians donate old
master paintings to the Museum. Governor and Mrs. Luther H. Hodges donate
funds for the acquisition of one of a pair
of English portraits, *Lady Cavendish, Later
Countess of Devonshire, and her Daughter*,
by Paul van Somer. With funds contributed by John Motley Morehead, the
Museum acquires the pendant portrait
*William, Lord Cavendish, Later Second Earl
of Devonshire, and his Son*, also by van
Somer. Valentiner had located the por-

traits on the London art market and recommended them for the Museum's collection. Mr. and Mrs. Ralph Price of
Greensboro give the Museum funds to
acquire another important painting, *Portrait of a Gentleman*, by the Dutch artist
Anthonis Mor.

*On September 20, the University of
North Carolina at Chapel Hill dedicates the
William Hayes Ackland Art Center on the
university campus. Joseph C. Sloane is the
Ackland Art Center's first director.*

In November, Edwin Gill receives
$8,000 from the North Carolina Council
of State to allow sponsorship of a memorial exhibition in honor of Valentiner.

1959 Eight years after the Kress Foundation pledge of $1 million in works of art,
the State Art Commission accepts the
foundation's gift of sixty-nine paintings
and two sculptures — now valued at $2.5
million.[42] The Kress donation includes an
important group of paintings by four-
teenth-century Italian masters, most
notably the *Peruzzi Altarpiece* by Giotto
and his workshop, as well as works from
the fifteenth through the eighteenth centuries. These masterpieces of Italian
painting and sculpture fill an intentional
gap in the collection: knowing that the
Kress Collection was rich in early Italian
paintings, the Art Commission had limited its purchases of such works with the
original state appropriation. The Kress

collection also includes ten paintings from the French, Dutch, Flemish, and German schools.

On April 6, the *Valentiner Memorial Exhibition: Masterpieces of Art* opens. The 117 works displayed include loans from all of the museums that Valentiner directed: the Detroit Institute of Arts, the Los Angeles County Museum, and the J. Paul Getty Museum. The exhibition also includes other loans from the United States, Canada, and Europe. When it closes on May 17, the exhibition has drawn some 28,500 visitors — a new attendance record for the Museum.

Works of art valued at more than $250,000 are donated in honor of Valentiner, including a French, late thirteenth-century ivory sculpture, *Madonna and Child*, a gift of Mrs. Edsel B. Ford of Detroit, and a watercolor, *Factory*, by Lyonel Feininger, a gift of the artist's widow. Other gifts include a Flemish pen and watercolor drawing attributed to Jan Breughel the Elder, *Sketches of Cattle and Farmers*, gift of Julius Böhler; and a Dutch painting attributed to Jan Lievens, *Fantastic Landscape*, a contribution from Morton D. May.

As a further tribute to Valentiner, a painting that he had discovered on his last trip to London is acquired by public subscription. *St. Matthew and the Angel*, by Willem Drost, is purchased partially with a memorial fund. In addition, friends of Valentiner are invited to help acquire the painting by purchasing one-inch squares of a scale drawing of the painting, which had been divided into 1700 squares valued at ten dollars each.[43]

The North Carolina General Assembly appropriates $624,000 to construct an addition to the Museum. Governor Luther H. Hodges appoints five members of the Art Society board of directors to a building committee to consider whether to construct a wing or an addition.

The staff and the volunteer groups continue to grow in number. In addition to a curator of education, employed in 1958, the Museum employs a public information officer and a photographer. Volunteer guides number sixty-five, including members of the Raleigh Junior League and the Raleigh Junior Woman's Clubs.

Members of the Sir Walter Cabinet (wives of members of the state legislature and of other state officials) begin a series of lectures. Charles Stanford, curator of education, conducts the lecture series.

1960 In March, the Museum names James B. Byrnes interim director. Governor Hodges, who also serves as honorary president of the Art Society, requests that Byrnes remain until the governor's term expires at the end of the year. In the meantime, the Art Society board of directors continues its search to fill the director's position.

In May, total attendance at the Museum since its opening in April 1956 reaches 250,000 visitors.

In June, the Museum opens the exhibition *Modern French Art — From Monet to Picasso*, from the Maurice Wertheim Collection. Among the forty works shown are paintings, drawings, and sculpture, including works by Cézanne, Gauguin,

Maillol, Matisse, Monet, Picasso, and Va Gogh.

The North Carolina State Art Societ names Justus Bier as its choice for Muse um director. Bier is head of the art depart ment of the University of Louisville i Kentucky. He assumes his new position i January 1961.

On November 30, the ribbon is cut fo the long-awaited public opening of th Kress galleries. Concerns for the preserva tion and safety of a priceless art collec tion, housed in a recently renovated stat office building, had delayed the opening Governor Hodges accepted the collectio for the Museum — and for the people c North Carolina.

Byrnes resigns as interim director a

"From the point of view of the Samuel H. Kress Foundation, the creation of the North Carolina Museum of Art inspires particular pride, since it is arguable that the new state museum in Raleigh actually came into being as a result of Kress philanthropy."
— Marilyn Perry, president of the Samuel H. Kress Foundation

1.　　Mrs. Robert Lee Humber pours tea for members of the Sir Walter Cabinet in 1959. Reprinted by permission of the NC Division of Archives and History and *The News & Observer* of Raleigh, North Carolina.

2.　　Edwin Gill (far end of table) addresses the Museum board of trustees at a 1959 meeting to select a new director. Reprinted by permission of the NC Division of Archives and History and *The News & Observer* of Raleigh, North Carolina.

3.　　Education Director Charles Stanford speaks with a group of Museum docents in 1959.

3.

the end of the year. The Art Society passes a resolution praising his contributions to organizing educational programs at the Museum and for his efforts in bringing "many and valuable gifts to the Museum ranging over the history of art from ancient Egyptian, Greek and Roman times, down to the art of our own day."[44]

THE MATURING MUSEUM, 1961 – 1969

"I constantly cited our Museum of Art in recruiting
new industries. It is indeed one of our great state treasures."
—Terry Sanford, Chairman of the Museum Board
of Trustees and Governor of North Carolina, 1961–65

1961 – 1964 Justus Bier, an authority on the late-Gothic German master sculptor Tilmann Riemenschneider, becomes Museum director. During his tenure at the University of Louisville, 1939 – 1961, Bier created the Allen R. Hite Art Institute, a well-known teaching museum.

With the arrival of its new director, the NCMA begins to expand its sculpture collection. One addition is *Madonna and Child Sheltering Supplicants Under her Cloak*, attributed to Peter Köellin, a German sculptor of the Swabian School.

Before his death, Valentiner had selected for acquisition a painting by Flemish artist Theodor Rombouts, *The Backgammon Players*, and the painting *Portrait of a Gentleman*, by Bernardo Strozzi. Through the influence of Robert Lee Humber and Rachel Maxwell Moore, a member of the Art Society board of directors from Greenville, North Carolina, several Greenville art patrons purchase the paintings. The Museum also acquires the twelfth-century French sculpture *Madonna and Child Enthroned*, which Valentiner had borrowed earlier for an exhibition.

Benefactors purchase two works from Valentiner's estate: the painting *Young Shepherd with a Flower*, by Ernst Ludwig Kirchner, given anonymously; and a bronze sculpture, *Portrait of W. R. Valentiner*, by Georg Kolbe, gift of Mr. and Mrs. Ralph Hanes, Jr., and Mr. and Mrs. Calder Womble.

The General Assembly establishes the North Carolina Museum of Art as an independent state agency, thus separating it from the North Carolina State Art Society. The General Assembly creates a board of trustees with ultimate responsibility for the Museum, its acquisitions, and the development of its programs. Four members of the board will be elected by the Art Society's directors.

In compliance with the legislative Act of 1961, the State Art Society transfers all of its art holdings — including the works purchased with funds from the 1947 legislative appropriation, the Kress Foundation gift, its collection of works by North Carolina artists, and the Phifer Collection — to the NCMA. The society, however,

1.	Justus Bier at the 1962 *Riemenschneider* exhibition with Marilyn Stokstad, director of the University of Kansas Museum of Art.

2.	*Madonna and Child Sheltering Supplicants under Her Cloak,* attributed to Peter Köellin, added to the Museum's growing sculpture collection.

3.	Chief Curator Ben Williams visits the Riemenschneider exhibition. Reprinted by permission of the NC Division of Archives and History and *The News & Observer* of Raleigh, North Carolina.

continues to administer funds it receives from the Phifer Bequest.

Robert Lee Humber, addressing the annual meeting of the Art Society in November, says the fact that the state is assuming full responsibility for the operation of the Museum is a tribute to the society's efforts. He encourages the group to continue its work in initiating arts projects throughout the state.[45]

Governor Terry Sanford (1961 – 65) appoints Humber chairman of the North Carolina Museum of Art Board of Trustees.

Joseph C. Sloane, director of the Ackland Art Museum and head of the art department at the University of North Carolina at Chapel Hill, becomes the Art Society's fourth president. He is the first person from the professional art field to hold the position.

In December, the North Carolina Museum of Art officially receives title to the Kress Collection, during ceremonies at Washington's National Gallery of Art. The Kress Foundation's gift includes funds for the continuous care, treatment, restoration, and framing needs of the collection.[46]

Director Bier organizes the exhibition *Sculptures of Tilmann Riemenschneider,* which brings international attention to the NCMA. The exhibition is the first held outside of Germany that is devoted to the work of this German Gothic master. Works on loan include those from the Louvre, Paris; the Rijksmuseum, Amster-dam; several museums and private collections in Germany; and the Metropolitan Museum of Art, New York. The exhibition catalogue contains the first survey of the life of Riemenschneider published in English.

With funds from the Mary Duke Biddle Foundation, the Museum acquires the German sculpture *Adoring Angel.*

In October, Governor Terry Sanford opens a statewide conference on "Responsibility for Aesthetic Quality" with a message from President John F. Kennedy: "The North Carolina Museum of Art has been foremost among those which effectively combine private support with the support of the state government."[47]

The General Assembly provides addi-

tional support for scholarly publications and educational programs. It appropriates money to again publish the *North Carolina Museum of Art Bulletin*, after a four-year lapse.

Funding by the state for the art purchase fund enables the NCMA to acquire a major French eighteenth-century painting by Jean-Baptiste-Siméon Chardin, *Still Life with Ray and Basket of Onions*.

The Art Society, under the leadership of President Sloane, successfully explores ways to combine its support of the Museum and other state art programs, resulting in the establishment of regional art representatives in some areas of the state.

Through the efforts of two Art Society representatives in Winston-Salem,

Ruth Julian and Smith Bagley, the NCMA and the society organize the exhibition *Collectors' Opportunity*. The Museum borrows works from galleries in New York, hoping to interest more North Carolinians in art and encourage them to become collectors. Director Bier and Art Society President Sloane serve as advisors for the project.

In December, the Art Society begins to donate works of art, selected from the annual *North Carolina Artist's Exhibition*, to other state galleries and museums. It continues to offer the NCMA its choice of award-winning *NCAE* works.

Humber, chairman of the North Carolina Museum of Art Board of Trustees, proposes some new ideas for boosting

financial support. The trustees submit a charter and bylaws to the state attorney general to establish the North Carolina Museum of Art Foundation. The board names Mary Semans, Ralph Price, Egbert L. Davis, Jr., and Edwin M. Gill charter members of the foundation. (The foundation receives its charter in December 1969.)

The NCMA continues to organize contemporary art exhibitions. Curator Benjamin F. Williams travels to London and assembles the work of six artists for the 1964 *Young British Painters* exhibition, which is later shown in Winston-Salem and Wilmington.

Governor Terry Sanford establishes, by executive order, the North Carolina Arts

4.	George Bireline with his painting *Red Shift* selected by the Art Society for the permanent collection from the 1964 *North Carolina Artists Exhibition*.

5.	Curator Ben Williams (right) and a juror consider works submitted for the 1961 *North Carolina Artists Exhibition*.

6.	Beth Cummings Paschal (Art Society president, 1964 – 1967) and Joseph C. Sloane (Art Society president, 1961 – 1964).

Photos 4 – 6 reprinted by permission of the NC Division of Archives and History and *The News & Observer* of Raleigh, North Carolina.

5.

6.

48–49

Council and appoints R. Philip Hanes, Jr., chairman.

In 1963, Governor Sanford supports legislation to establish the North Carolina School of the Arts in Winston-Salem — the first state-supported, residential school for performing arts in the nation. The school opens in 1965.

2.

1.

1965 – 1966 Seven years after the death of Director Valentiner, the NCMA receives from his estate eighty-five works: paintings, drawings, and sculpture.[48]

Valentiner had bequeathed his entire art collection to the Museum, but his former wife contested the will. After reaching a settlement with Mrs. Valentiner, the Museum received a share of the collection. The NCMA's German Expressionist collection today consists largely of works from Valentiner's collection.

Two new programs developed by the Education Department are announced. Education Curator Charles Stanford, with assistance from Priscilla Sprunt of Raleigh and others, initiates a pilot study devised to help the visually impaired learn about art through the sense of touch. The new education gallery for the visually impaired opens in 1966. The first gallery of its type in an American museum, it receives national and international attention. NBC Television features the gallery in one of its programs. The Mary Duke Biddle Foundation donates funds for the gallery, and the Museum names the new facility the Mary Duke Biddle Gallery.

The Education Department begins a series of slide programs supported by a grant from the Junior League of Raleigh.

By 1966, the docent program numbers 140 volunteers, enrolled for the first time in two training programs for beginning and advanced docents.

One of the Museum's major exhibitions in 1966 features drawings by John White of the first English colony in the New World. White illustrated early colonial life on Roanoke Island, home of the Lost Colony. Some of his illustrations survived and ultimately were acquired by the British Museum in 1866.[49] Curator Benjamin Williams had negotiated with the British Museum and arranged for the surviving 113 drawings to be returned to North Carolina to be exhibited for the first time in the United States. Following their presentation at the NCMA, the National Gallery and the Pierpont Morgan Library in New York also show the drawings.

Purchase of the Raphael painting *St. Jerome Punishing the Heretic Sabinian* is made possible with funds from the Sarah

4.

the flyer.

3.

"Loath to overlook an opportunity to celebrate, in 1967 the Museum recognized the twentieth anniversary of the $1 million appropriation with a grand reception for the state legislature, and with a year-long series of Community Days, inviting any community in the state to have its own day in the Museum."
— Beth Cummings Paschal

Graham Kenan Foundation, Mrs. Nancy Susan Reynolds, Julius H. Weitzner, and the State of North Carolina.

In April 1966, Governor Dan K. Moore (1965 – 69) issues an executive order to re-establish the North Carolina Arts Council and again names R. Philip Hanes, Jr., as chairman.

1967 The North Carolina Museum of Art celebrates the twentieth anniversary of its founding.

The State Art Society, under the leadership efforts of its fifth president, Beth Cummings Paschal, begins to expand its programs.

Many gifts and purchases of works of art distinguish the Museum's anniversary year. North Carolina National Bank (now NationsBank) and Wachovia Bank lend French Impressionist paintings. North Carolina National Bank lends *Trouville, the Jetties, High Tide*, by Eugène-Louis Boudin; Wachovia Bank lends *The Saint Sever Bridge from Rouen, Fog*, by Camille Pissarro. Both benefactors later give the paintings to the Museum. The Art Society

donates a pastel by Edgar Degas, *Le Repos*.

In special recognition of the twentieth anniversary, the General Assembly appropriates $50,000 for the Museum's art purchase fund. These additional funds enable the purchase of *The Cliff, Etretat, Sunset*, by Claude Monet, and a portrait painting, *Dr. Albert C. Getchell*, by Thomas Eakins.

Supporters and private collectors are honored with the exhibition *North Carolina Collects*. Accompanied by a comprehensive catalogue, the exhibition includes 274 works of art from 124 collectors.

Due to the continuing efforts of Governor Moore, Dr. Humber, and the board of trustees, the General Assembly acknowledges the need for a new building and

creates the Art Museum Building Commission. On July 5, 1967, the North Carolina General Assembly enacts into law and ratifies the Act to Create the State Art Museum Building Commission and to Provide for the Erection of a State Art Museum Building.[50]

State Senator Thomas J. White of Kinston led the effort to create the commission, which includes fifteen members appointed by the governor, president of the state senate, and speaker of the house of representatives. Governor Moore appoints Senator White chairman of the commission.[51] The commission's many duties include choosing a site, selecting architects, approving plans and drawings, and contracting for building construction, fur-

nishings, and equipment.

For the anniversary year, the State Art Society initiates two successful programs. Community Days at the NCMA encourages first-time and regular visitors to come to the Museum to receive a special welcome from officials, legislators, and members of the Art Society. As a result of Community Days visits, at least one group raises money to enable the purchase of a twentieth-century watercolor: The Chapel Hill chapter of the North Carolina State Art Society gives *Schnee Wetter*, by Georg Grosz.

Beth Cummings Paschal, president of the society, develops and expands the volunteer program. Volunteers now help receive visitors, staff the information desk

and bookshop, coordinate hospitality activities, and serve as staff aides for the Curatorial and Public Relations departments.

The Art Society inaugurates a Collectors Circle and continues its support of the *North Carolina Artists Exhibition* and Museum receptions. Mariana T. Manning, a long-time member of the society, assists with organizing the annual exhibition for many years.

The Art Society also provides a kit containing slides and lecture text for schools, libraries, and civic groups. It sponsors art teacher study tours and traveling exhibitions for regional galleries. According to Paschal, in an article to commemorate the Museum's twentieth anniversary,

3.

she wrote: "These are other ways the State Art Society chooses to promote art in general and the North Carolina Museum of Art in particular. The society has . . . a mission to make North Carolinians realize that the North Carolina Museum of Art is one of the proudest possessions of the State and that it should be cherished and used by all."[52]

Museum attendance and the number of guided tours continue to increase, with 80,000 visitors recorded in 1967.

The North Carolina Arts Council becomes a permanent state agency, following action by the General Assembly.

1.

1968 – 1969 Renovation of the third and fourth floors provides additional, flexible space for the permanent collection, special exhibitions, and the Mary Duke Biddle Gallery. Four large windows facing the street on the first floor are removed and filled in, improving security and increasing exhibition space. Staff offices, the State Art Society office, and the Museum library move to the sixth floor of the adjacent highway building annex.

Acquisitions continue to expand the sculpture collection. With art purchase funds provided by the state and the Phifer Bequest, the Museum acquires a rare sculpture of a female saint, by Tilmann Riemenschneider. The acquisition is a tribute to Director Bier's insight and profound knowledge of this late Gothic master. In honor of its second president, Katherine Pendleton Arrington, the Art Society provides Phifer Bequest funds for the acquisition of a Greek marble *Torso of Aphrodite*.

In honor of Robert Lee Humber, Mr. and Mrs. Charles Lee Smith, Jr., contribute funds in 1968 for the purchase of a historically important silver tea and coffee service, by American craftsman Anthony Rasch.

The National Endowment for the Arts announces a program to help museums acquire works of art by living American artists. The program offers a $10,000 grant, provided the recipient matches the funds. The Art Society matches the NEA grant with funds from the Phifer Bequest, and the North Carolina Museum of Art is among the first fifteen museums in the country to become eligible for NEA funding through this program. In 1969, the Museum makes the first purchases: an Alexander Calder mobile, *Tricolor on Pyramid*, and a painted sculpture, *Open Column*, by Ilya Bolotowsky. The liaison between the NEA and the society continues, enabling the Museum to expand its contemporary collection.53

Opening in early 1969 is the contemporary exhibition *American Abstract Artists*, which focuses on trends in American abstract art since 1936 and includes the work of thirty-six artists, including Josef Albers and Ilya Bolotowsky, both of whom taught at Black Mountain College.

2.

The NCMA Education Department continues to develop new programs and activities. Charles Stanford, curator of education, initiates lectures for the deaf — the first museum program of this type in the nation. Assisting Stanford are Mrs. William P. Davis of Sanford and Mrs. Charles M. Reeves, Jr., of Southern Pines. Davis and Reeves learn sign language and teach docents the language. (The State Art Society elects Reeves president in 1977.)

The Mary Duke Biddle Gallery opens the exhibition *Kinetic Art*, which includes twenty-one works of art by Willi Gutmann, Ernest Trova, François Baschet, and Bernard Baschet.

Charles Stanford receives the North Carolina Award for Fine Arts. The citation, presented by Governor Robert W. Scott (1969 – 1973), states that Stanford "has become the architect of an enduring contribution to civilization."

In 1969, the North Carolina General Assembly makes its first appropriation, $3 million, to construct a new building for the North Carolina Museum of Art.

GROWTH AND DIVERSIFICATION, 1970 – 1980

"My first visit when I arrived in Raleigh, in 1971, was to the Museum, and there I felt the full impact of Southern friendliness and acceptance that has been my joy ever since."

—*Dr. Abram Kanof, Museum Trustee Emeritus and adjunct curator of the Judaic collection*

1970 Justus Bier, director since January 1961, retires effective April 1, 1970, and is appointed curator of research and director emeritus. Duke University presents Bier an honorary Doctor of Fine Arts degree shortly after he resigns the director's position.[54]

Charles W. Stanford, curator of education since 1958, is appointed as the new director.

The Museum receives its one millionth visitor.

On November 10, Robert Lee Humber dies at the age of seventy-two. "A Resolution Honoring the Life and Memory of Robert Lee Humber" reads in part: "Robert Lee Humber set forth with high purpose on a quest to improve the quality of cul-

tural life in North Carolina and with single-minded zeal, determined vitality and a glowing sense of adventure he reached this goal by pioneering the acquisition of a great Museum of Art . . . . we pay loving tribute to his memory and forever keep his image bright . . . . we vow to continue his magnificent quest to make North Carolina one of the cultural centers of the world."[55]

On November 18, Governor Scott appoints Egbert L. Davis, Jr., chairman of the Museum board of trustees.

1971 The Museum embarks on the initial phase of a major project to document the visual arts program at Black Mountain College. The intent is to publish a documentary catalogue and organize a major exhibition designed to present the history, contribution, and significance of the college in the history of twentieth-century American art. Private funds provided by the Mary Duke Biddle Foundation, the Mary Reynolds Babcock Foundation, Thomas S. Kenan III, and Gordon Hanes support the initial phase of the project.

After interviewing representatives from forty-three firms, the State Art Museum Building Commission selects the architects to design the new museum building. The New York firm of Edward

"Dr. Humber came one afternoon and it was early evening when he left. We were inspired beyond any measure by his description of his decision after World War II to put the funding he had accumulated into developing a museum of art in Raleigh and to pour his whole life into it. He cared more about great art than anyone I have ever, ever known."
— Mary Semans, first president of the NCMA Foundation and former Museum trustee

1.

1.   Members of the Museum building commission with (starting third from left) Charles Stanford, Senator Thomas White, and Robert L. Humber in 1970.

2.   Charles Stanford, Museum director, and Moussa Domit, associate director, discuss building plans for the North Carolina Museum of Art.

2.

56–57

Durrell Stone and Associates is chosen, along with Holloway-Reeves Architects of Raleigh as associate architects. Stone and Associates had previously designed the Kennedy Center in Washington, the Museum of Modern Art in New York, and the North Carolina Legislative Building in Raleigh.

The Executive Organization Act of 1971 transfers the North Carolina Museum of Art, the Museum board of trustees, the State Art Society, and the Art Museum Building Commission to the newly created Department of Art, Culture, and History. The new department, headed by a state cabinet-level secretary appointed by the governor, is the first agency of its kind in the nation.[56] Governor Scott appoints

Samuel T. Ragan — a well-known newspaper editor, writer, and recipient of the North Carolina Tercentenary Poetry Award in 1963 — as secretary.

Given by Mr. and Mrs. Fabius B. Pendleton are a pastel painting, *Tobacco Patch*, by John Henry Twachtman, and a bronze sculpture, *The Puritan*, by Augustus Saint-Gaudens, both formerly in the collection of Katherine Pendleton Arrington.

The North Carolina General Assembly appropriates an additional $1 million for the construction of a new museum.

1.

2.

1.   *Lucius Caesar*, a Roman marble sculpture given by Dr. and Mrs. George W. Paschal, Jr., helped expand the classical collection.

2.   *Cebolla Church* by Georgia O'Keeffe was purchased in 1972 in honor of Joseph Sloane.

3.   The Museum and the Art Society sponsored a 1973 exhibition of paintings acquired through the generosity of Robert F. Phifer.

4.   Exhibitions in 1973 included *North Carolina Craftsmen*.

3.

1972   In January, the NCMA selects Moussa M. Domit as associate director. At the time of his selection, Domit is a curator at the National Gallery of Art, and was formerly associate director at the Corcoran Gallery of Art in Washington. He had been considered for the director's position prior to the selection of Charles W. Stanford.

Domit is chiefly responsible for the pre-architectural program for a museum building — a document he and the Museum staff write.[57]

The collection begins to expand through the interest and generosity of Mr. and Mrs. Gordon Hanes of Winston-Salem, the James G. Hanes Memorial Fund, and the Art Society. Works of art are also acquired with state art purchase funds. These acquisitions include expansion into areas of non-western art — Egyptian, Greek, Roman, New World, and African art. A Roman marble sculpture, *Lucius Caesar*, a gift from Dr. and Mrs. George W. Paschal, Jr., adds to the developing classical collection. There are also additions to the collection of American late nineteenth-and twentieth-century art.

The State Art Society honors two members by providing funds to purchase *Cebolla Church*, by Georgia O'Keeffe, in honor of Joseph C. Sloane, and *Dorothy, Helen, and Bob*, by William Merritt Chase, in honor of Edwin Gill.

Ola Maie Foushee releases her book Art in North Carolina: Episodes and Developments, 1585 to 1970.

4.

1973 The General Assembly allocates $200,000 for the purchase of works of art.

With the Executive Organization Act of 1973, the Department of Art, Culture, and History becomes the Department of Cultural Resources. At the same time, the act abolishes the board of trustees and replaces it with an art commission that reports to and consults with the Secretary of the Department of Cultural Resources.

Governor James E. Holshouser Jr. (1973 – 77), appoints Joseph C. Sloane chairman of the new Museum Art Commission. Sloane, a professor of art at UNC-Chapel Hill and past president of the Art Society from 1961 – 64, remains chairman until 1980, when the General Assembly

reestablishes a board of trustees as the Museum's governing body.

The Act of 1973 also renames the State Art Museum Building Commission; the word "State" is deleted. Although the duties and responsibilities of the commission remain basically the same, a requirement is added that the site of the new museum building must be selected in accordance with directions, if any, from the General Assembly.

The North Carolina General Assembly appropriates funds for a full-time conservator and for the establishment of a conservation laboratory. Until now the Museum has relied on private, out-of-state conservators for its conservation needs. An NEA grant helps fund a muse-

um program to survey the conservation needs of the collection and to develop proposals for the establishment of conservation studios, both for the present museum site and the new museum.

The NCMA receives accreditation by the American Association of Museums.

The docents group of the North Carolina Museum of Art formally organizes.

Exhibitions during 1973 include *North Carolina Arts and Crafts*, co-sponsored by the NCMA and the North Carolina Arts Council.

The Museum and the Art Society jointly sponsor an exhibition and catalogue of the Robert F. Phifer Collection. Benjamin F. Williams, head curator, organizes the exhibition, which includes

1.

approximately fifty paintings from Robert Phifer's personal collection, as well as paintings acquired with funds from the Phifer Bequest.58

The Art Society inaugurates an annual Beaux-Arts Ball. Chaired by Beth Cummings Paschal, the first ball takes place in Southern Pines.

The North Carolina General Assembly appropriates an additional $4.5 million for the construction of a new museum.

1974 – 1976 Charles Stanford resigns in late 1973 after a serious injury, and Moussa M. Domit becomes director in June 1974.

The Museum continues to strengthen its collection in the areas of Egyptian, classical, and New World art, established largely by gifts in the previous two years, and acquires major new works with the state art purchase fund. With state funds, it purchases the American twentieth-century painting *Indian Fantasy*, by Marsden Hartley. Two gifts from the Sarah Graham Kenan Foundation add to the French Impressionist and American nineteenth-century collection. *The Seine at Giverny, Morning Mists*, by Claude Monet, is a gift of the Kenan Foundation and the Art Society (Phifer Bequest). *Lotus Flowers: A Land-scape Painting in the Background*, by Martin J. Heade, is also a gift of the Kenan Foundation in honor of Mrs. Sarah Graham Kenan. In recognition of Beth Cummings Paschal, one of its past presidents, the State Art Society purchases *Sunset (Medusa)*, by Russian-American painter Eugene Berman.

The Museum receives as a gift from the North Carolina Citizens Association the portrait painting *Benjamin Franklin*, by Joseph-Siffred Duplessis. R. J. Reynolds Industries gives a portrait, *Sea Dog*, by American artist Andrew Wyeth. The state library of North Carolina transfers to the Museum a four-volume, rare first edition of *The Birds of America*, by John James Audubon59 and a three-volume set of

2.

3.

4.

1.   The State Art Society purchased Eugene Berman's *Sunset (Medusa)* in recognition of the contributions of Beth Cummings Paschal.

2.   Mrs. Isaac Manly (Art Society President, 1974 – 1976) and Dr. Manly enjoy *American Impressionism* in 1974.

3.   Dr. Abram Kanof (foreground) explains a detail at *Ceremonial Art in the Judaic Tradition*.

4.   The *Eugene Ruhkin* exhibition in 1975 combined abstraction with traditional Russian iconography.

"My most satisfying work with the Museum was raising the funds from my business associates to purchase the Duplessis painting of Benjamin Franklin for the bicentennial of the United States."
— *Ivie L. Clayton, NCMA Foundation president and Museum trustee*

Audubon's *Viviparous Quadrupeds of America*.

NCMA exhibitions during this period include *American Impressionist Painting*, curated by Moussa Domit in cooperation with the National Gallery of Art; *Ceremonial Art in the Judaic Tradition*, organized by the Museum and guest curator Dr. Abram Kanof; and *Eugene Rukhin, a Contemporary Russian Painter*, organized by Domit.

The *American Impressionist Painting* exhibition debuts at the National Gallery of Art in Washington, then travels to the Whitney Museum of American Art in New York and the Cincinnati Art Museum before opening at the NCMA in the spring of 1974.

In 1974, the Museum agrees to co-sponsor a collectors gallery. The gallery's purpose is to exhibit and offer works of art — created mostly by North Carolina artists — to the public for purchase or rental. The Museum's curatorial staff advises the gallery manager.[60]

In 1974, the North Carolina General Assembly appropriates an additional $2.25 million for the construction of a new museum.

Ceremonial Art in the Judaic Tradition, in 1975, is one of the most ambitious exhibitions yet organized by the Museum and includes approximately two hundred objects related to the celebration of the Jewish faith. The exhibition becomes the stimulus to establish a permanent collection of Judaic art.

The *Eugene Rukhin* exhibition, which opens in autumn 1975, is the first major showing of the work of that contemporary Russian artist by an American museum and receives national media coverage.

The thirty-eighth annual *North Carolina Artists Exhibition* is on view during November and December of 1975 and includes crafts for the first time. From a total of ninety-eight works of art shown, thirty-eight are crafts.

The NCMA and the Art Society co-sponsor an exhibition, *200 Years of the Visual Arts in North Carolina*, commemorating the nation's bicentennial anniversary. Curator Benjamin F. Williams and Dorothy B. Rennie, head of the Museum's

2.

1.

"The Building Commission appeared before a legislative committee to defend its position. At one such meeting, the widow of Governor Broughton appeared on behalf of the downtown site because, in her opinion, our site was too far away. State Treasurer Edwin Gill answered saying, 'Alice, I could drive by your house and take you to our Museum in ten minutes.'"
— Mary Semans

programs research and coordination branch, are organizers.

In 1976, the North Carolina State Art Society celebrates its fiftieth anniversary. The society continues to sponsor education and fund-raising events, including art kits for schools and libraries, Community Days, art travel tours, the Beaux-Arts Ball, and the collectors gallery.

Another exhibition, which opens at the end of 1976 and brings national media coverage to the Museum, is *Correspondence: An Exhibition of the Letters of Ray Johnson*. The show features mail art by Johnson, a well-known artist who founded the New York Correspondence School. Hundreds of artists participated in Johnson's school, as the show clearly illus-

trates. The exhibition, organized by Huston Paschal, assistant to the head of the programs research branch, and Richard Craven, associate head of the educational services branch, is the first museum display of Johnson's correspondence and includes more than five hundred items. The accompanying catalogue published by the Museum contains reproductions of approximately two hundred of Johnson's letters.

From 1974 to 1976, the Museum receives several grants and additional state funds. The NEA awards $10,000 for the purchase of works by living American artists, an amount which the Art Society matches. The NEA also awards a grant to support research and publication of a cat-

alogue of the Museum's Dutch and Flemish collections. Another NEA grant enables the Museum to survey the regional conservation needs and examine the feasibility of establishing a regional conservation facility in the new building.

Through the efforts of Edwin Gill, the Council of State funds two NCMA requests for operational assistance. In 1975, funds were authorized to upgrade the Museum's security and fire protection systems. In 1976, the council approves funds to purchase the necessary equipment for the newly established conservation laboratory.

The National Endowment for the Humanities awards a grant to help implement an affiliate gallery network, consist-

4.

1 – 2. *200 Years of the Visual Arts in North Carolina* included views of architecture in styles from Colonial to contemporary.

3. Bluegrass musicians perform at the opening of the bicentennial exhibition.

4. (left to right) Ben Williams, Sherman Lee, Mrs. Isaac Manly and Dr. Manly at the 38th *North Carolina Artists Exhibition*.

5. Exhibition organizers Huston Paschal (left) and Richard Craven (right) with artist Ray Johnson at the 1976 opening of *Correspondence: An Exhibition of the Letters of Ray Johnson*.

5.

ing of twelve member art museums. The grant will pay the salary of a full-time program coordinator for one year. The NCMA will provide services to galleries in other parts of the state; however, no direct financial aid is provided. Instead, the Museum will lend works of art from its collection for both short- and long-term exhibitions. In addition, the program will provide technical consultation services for exhibitions and other programs. After the one-year grant period, state funds support the program for another decade. In 1987, the member galleries vote to disband.

Controversy surrounding the selection of a site delays construction of the new building. During the earlier selection process, the site selection committee had studied all available land owned by the State of North Carolina in Raleigh and its environs. The committee obtained the services of an out-of-state consulting firm, which provided data about traffic patterns, population trends, and other matters related to site selection. The firm then made several recommendations, but stated a preference for a site located on Blue Ridge Road on the western edge of Raleigh.

The building commission had approved the site in 1972, as had the State Capital Planning Commission. In early 1973, the governor and the Council of State also give their approval.

From 1973 to 1975, public opposition to the Blue Ridge Road site increases; opponents think the new museum should be downtown, near the Capitol and other public and historic buildings.

Wake County members of the General Assembly introduce bills requiring that the new museum be in downtown Raleigh. Others opposing the Blue Ridge Road site file a lawsuit in Wake County Superior Court. When the presiding judge dismisses the suit, they appeal to the Supreme Court of North Carolina, which upholds the authority of the State Art Museum Building commission to determine the site. All bills pending in the legislature challenging the commission's site selection are killed in committee.[61]

Because of the delay caused by the

1.   Moussa Domit (kneeling), with (left to right) Roy Lawrence, Beth Cummings Paschal, Mrs. Dan K. Moore, Gordon Hanes, and Joseph C. Sloane at the construction site in 1977.

2.   Duane Hanson sculptures fooled the eye during *Eight Contemporary American Realists* in 1977.

"Later, I was elected to the Art Museum Building Commission. That was a fascinating experience. We selected the architect and the site and visited great museums worldwide, using funds provided by a private grant from the Hanes Foundation."
— Thomas S. Kenan III

"The Museum board of trustees included people from all parts of the state . . . . The board took the point of view and they were exactly right, in my opinion — this is a state museum; it is not a Raleigh museum, it is not a Wake County museum . . . . we want to do all we possibly can to get the citizens — the young people and the elderly people, alike—to come from all over the state for their edification. We want a spacious atmosphere, a spacious amphitheater, a place to feel comfortable, not crowded, where other cultural activities can take place."
— Egbert L. Davis, Jr.

site debate, as well as continuing escalation of prices and inflation, the commission realizes that the $10.75 million appropriated by the state legislature is not sufficient to construct the new museum.[62] Building Commission president Thomas J. White appoints a finance committee, which, together with members of the Museum Art Commission, the Art Society, and the Museum Foundation, organizes a campaign to raise needed funds. Louis C. Stephens, Jr., president of Pilot Life Insurance Company in Greensboro, agrees to be campaign chairman. Beth Cummings Paschal becomes vice-chairman.[63]

Responding to the commission's efforts to raise private funds, the Art Society and the North Carolina Museum of Art Foundation, in September 1976, create a joint position of director of development for the Museum and administrative director of the Art Society. Roy Lawrence, a North Carolinian with experience in national and international finance administration, accepts the appointment.

1977 Construction of the new museum begins in July 1977.

That same year, the General Assembly amends the statutes pertaining to the North Carolina State Art Society by deleting the word "State" from the society's official title.

The General Assembly appropriates funds for the first "grass-roots arts program" in the nation. Local arts programs will receive state money on a per-capita basis.[64]

The Museum's collection is rapidly expanding, and its exhibitions continue to draw record numbers of visitors. In fiscal year 1977–78, the Museum records its greatest attendance to date, with nearly 108,000 visitors. The immediate need for

new and larger museum building be-
omes obvious.

In September, Director Moussa Domit
jives his report to the members of the Art
ommission concerning the growth of
he NCMA's collection. Domit notes that
1 the biennium ending June 30, 1977, the
Museum purchased 17 works and ac-
uired 651 more through gifts valued at
pproximately $1.7 million. Purchases with
tate funds include a Sicilian *Funerary*
ase (Lebes) and the painting *Spring on*
he Missouri, by Thomas Hart Benton. Art
ociety (Phifer Bequest) funds purchase
he American nineteenth-century paint-
ig *Still Life with Fruit*, by Severen Roesen,
1 honor of Mr. and Mrs. Charles Lee
mith, Jr. Lee and Dona Bronson donate

Breached Beaver Dam, by the contemporary American landscape paint- er Neil
Welliver, in honor of Edwin Gill.

One of the most popular exhibitions
to date, shown in December, is *Eight Contemporary American Realists*.

1.　　　*A Survey of Zairian Art: the Bronson Collection* opened in April 1978.

2 – 5.　　　Governor Hunt attends the press conference in 1979 (2) at the conclusion of the campaign fund drive and construction on the new museum continues.

1978 In April, the exhibition *A Survey of Zairian Art: The Bronson Collection* opens, which includes more than two hundred objects. Written by Joseph Cornet, director general of the Institute of the National Museums of Zaire, the catalogue updates previous publications on sculptural art in Zaire. After closing at the NCMA, the exhibition travels to the Museum of African Art in Washington and the Los Angeles County Museum of Natural History.

In July 1978, the Museum loses a dear friend and loyal supporter with the death of Edwin Maurice Gill. The resolution to his memory adopted by the North Carolina Museum of Art Commission and written by Mary Semans states: "He inspired everyone around him with a particular affection for the Museum . . . . He reminded everyone that the whole of North Carolina was its constituency and urged that every school child in the state have a clear opportunity to participate in its programs and to learn about its holdings."

1979 – 1980 Work on the new museum and the campaign to raise money for its completion continue. The staff begin planning for the move, while maintaining programs and activities on Morgan Street. The volunteer and docent organizations continue to help during this transition period.

At this time, the NCMA staff request assistance from several specialists to help them plan the collection's move to the new building. Sherman Lee, director of The Cleveland Museum of Art, is asked to study and assess the oriental collection. Christopher White, director of the Ashmolean Museum, Oxford University, will study the collection of prints and drawings.

3.

4.

5.

Curator Benjamin Williams resigns in July 1979 to accept the position of Curator of Art at the newly created Visual Arts Center at North Carolina State University. A resolution written by Joseph C. Sloane to honor Williams for three decades of service reads in part: "During his tenure he arranged many special exhibitions . . . was in charge of the North Carolina Artist Competition, a major commitment to our native artists; gave frequent lectures, juried many art shows, and acted as consultant to audiences and arts organizations throughout the state and elsewhere . . . the Art Consultation Service of the Museum under his leadership rendered useful opinions about attribution, date, and authenticity of countless works of art

owned by private collectors."

Also in 1979, Patrick H. Sears, the Museum's first exhibition designer (1973 – 1976), assumes a newly created position related specifically to the move to the new building. Sears's task is to plan and coordinate the design and installation of the collection.

In December 1979, Louis C. Stephens, Jr., chairman of the Museum campaign to raise funds for the new building, announces that in slightly more than two years, the Museum has obtained donations totaling $5 million. Generous contributions have come from the Z. Smith Reynolds Foundation (a $1.5 million challenge grant), the William R. Kenan, Jr. Charitable Trust, and the Hanes Family

and Foundations. Other significant donations come from Mr. and Mrs. Warner L. Atkins, Irwin Belk, the Hanes Corporation, the Sarah Graham Kenan Foundation, and R. J. Reynolds Industries.

From late 1979 to May 1980, the Museum presents the final *Recent Acquisitions* exhibition in the downtown Museum. The exhibition includes both gifts and purchases — some of which will become major features when installed at the new Museum. Gifts from Gordon and Copey Hanes include the Egyptian wood sculpture *Striding Man*, and a Roman mosaic. The Hanes also give the Henry Moore sculpture *Large Spindle Piece*. Charles M. Reeves, Jr., and family donate an American Impressionist painting, *June Pastoral*, by

1.   Mr. and Mrs. Gordon
Hanes donated Henry Moore's *Large
Spindle Piece* to the NCMA in 1980.

2.

Willard Leroy Metcalf, in honor of Mrs. Charles M. Reeves, Jr., a past president of the Art Society.

With a grant from the NEA, matched by funds from the Art Society (Phifer Bequest), the NCMA acquires two works for the American twentieth-century collection: a sculpture by Louise Nevelson, *Black Zag CC*, and *Credit Blossom (Spread)*, by Robert Rauschenberg. With money from the state art purchase fund, the Museum purchases a Greek *Eye Cup* (Kylix), and a Roman funerary monument.

The forty-second *North Carolina Artists Exhibition* — the final *NCAE* held in the Morgan Street building — takes place in April 1980. The statistics include: 724 artists entering the competition, 474

paintings, 305 photographs, 158 sculptures, and 170 crafts. The total number of entries is 1,290, with 88 works by 84 artists selected.

In June 1980, Director Domit resigns, effective June 19 of that year. In December 1979, the Museum Art Commission had recognized Domit for his "contribution to the Museum's progress in all its programs." A listing of his accomplishments contained in the commission's affirmation includes improvement and development in the areas of collection preservation, security, research, exhibitions, exhibition design, publications, and the NCMA's building program. One of Domit's last official acts as director is to recommend the purchase of a Roman sculpture,

Aphrodite of Cyrene, after the Hellenistic original. State Art Society (Phifer Bequest) and state art purchase funds allow this acquisition, which is approved at the same commission meeting that Domit's resignation is accepted. Gay Hertzman, chief curator, becomes acting director.

Also in June 1980, the North Carolina General Assembly enacts legislation concerning the governing of the NCMA. It reestablishes the board of trustees as the Museum's governing body, and Governor James B. Hunt, Jr. (1977 – 1985) appoints Gordon Hanes chairman.

3.

68–69

1.

THE NEW NORTH CAROLINA MUSEUM OF ART, 1981 – 1985

"The four years [1981 to 1985] . . . were, without question, the most consequential years for the North Carolina Museum of Art since opening its doors in 1956."
—*Edgar Peters Bowron, Museum Director, 1981–85*

1981 – 1982 At its quarterly meeting in March of 1981, the board of trustees announces the appointment of Edgar Peters Bowron as director, effective May 1. Bowron is presently administrative assistant to the director and curator of Renaissance and Baroque art at The Nelson-Atkins Museum of Art in Kansas City, Missouri. He holds a doctoral degree in art history from the Institute of Fine Arts, New York University. Prior to his tenure at the Nelson-Atkins Museum, he was curator of Renaissance and Baroque art at the Walters Art Gallery in Baltimore.

On May 28, 1981, a dedication ceremony for the new building is held, followed by a reception and tour.

The tour reveals a beautiful new building — not yet a museum. Director Bowron, Associate Director Gay Hertzman, Chief Designer Patrick Sears, and the staff begin the transformation, estimating that it will take eighteen months to prepare for the public opening.

The staff must allocate gallery space for paintings and for the installation of the African, New World, Classical, and Egyptian collections. The director and the curatorial staff, together with Sears, decide where to construct partition walls. To provide sufficient space to install the collection, they must face some brick walls with a surface suitable for hanging works of art.

The design staff constructs custom display cases and designs gallery lighting.

They plan the layout of offices, art storage areas, packing and shipping spaces, conservation and photography laboratories, and the Nancy Susan Reynolds Education Wing.

The NCMA docent organization publishes a handbook for other museums planning to start docent programs. In the interval between closing the old building and opening the new one, docents participate in a vigorous outreach program to inform people about the new Museum. They travel to all areas of the state and speak to 3,500 people in more than 150 organizations.

In October 1981, the Museum and the Art Society co-sponsor a North Carolina Artists Symposium, "The Relationship of

2.

3.

4.

5.

1.   Art handlers Frank Manly and James McKeel prepare an Egyptian mummy case for packing.

2.   Registrar Peggy Jo D. Kirby (left) observes the packing of ancient sculptures while Chris Huber takes notes.

3.   Due to the lack of a loading dock, even the largest paintings in the collection had to go out of the front door at the old building.

4.   Installation of the Henry Moore sculpture in front of the new Museum.

5.   Director Edgar Peters Bowron (left) meets with the Steering Committee for the opening of the new building.

the Artist and the Art Museum in the 1980s," which replaces the annual *North Carolina Artists Exhibition* that year. The key issues for the symposium concern the NCMA's role in relation to the state's artists, the structure and design of the competition, and the relationship between crafts and other arts. The staff decides to present the next NCAE in the new building during the first year it is open to the public.

In January and February 1982, the staff begins moving from the Morgan Street building. The design and installation staffs relocate first. The library staff moves last, due to the specialized handling requirements of the library collection.

Meanwhile, the Morgan Street museum remains open to the public, but offers limited services. The permanent collection is no longer on view, as it is being prepared for the move. The collectors gallery, sponsored by the Art Society with curatorial and technical support from the staff, shows eleven exhibitions at the Morgan Street building from July 1981 until August 1982.

On August 31, 1982, the museum on Morgan Street closes to the public.

The continuing support of the General Assembly, Governor James B. Hunt, Jr., Secretary of Cultural Resources Sara W. Hodgkins, and Deputy Secretary Lawrence J. Wheeler enables the board of trustees, the director, and the staff to successfully

prepare for the opening of the new building.

The governor and the General Assembly significantly increase the budget for staff and administration from 1980 to 1983. Forty-two new positions, together with fifty-one positions already in the budget, provide resources to plan and complete the move.[65]

Between 1981 and 1983, Director Bowron appoints additional talented professionals: Sharon Broom, communications officer; William J. Chiego, chief curator; Joseph P. Covington, director of educational services; David C. Goist, chief conservator; James V. Hallsey, chief engineer; and Dare M. Hartwell, assistant conservator. Other appointees include Walter

1. Governor James Hunt
speaks at the dedication ceremony for
the new building.

2. Sen. Thomas White praises
the contributions of Building
Commission members, donors, and
Museum supporters.

3. Mr. and Mrs. Gordon
Hanes in front of Frank Stella's *Raqqa II*,
one of their many gifts to the Museum.

Jeffers, director of protection and custodi-al services; Mitchell D. Kahan, curator of American and contemporary art; Nancy B. Ketchiff, coordinator of adult programs; Mary Ellen Soles, curator of ancient art; David Steel, associate curator of European art; and Arete B. Swartz, assistant to the director. Swartz will also direct the newly established Development office in a position funded by the Mary Reynolds Babcock Foundation and the North Carolina Museum of Art Foundation.

Additions to the collection are numerous prior to the opening. Major gifts from two trustees enrich the European, ancient, and modern collections. Dr. and Mrs. Henry C. Landon donate *The Porcelain Collector*, by the Belgian artist

Alfred Stevens. Gordon and Copey Hanes donate two Egyptian sculptures: *Bust of the Goddess Sekhmet*, New Kingdom Dynasty XVIII, and *Model Boat with Figures*, Middle Kingdom Dynasty XII – XIII. They also purchase and donate two works for the American modern collection: *Pi*, by Morris Louis, and *Raqqa II*, by Frank Stella. Two purchases of European paintings from the late eighteenth century help fill gaps in that area of the collection. The George and Lucy Finch Trust Fund, the North Carolina Art Society (Phifer Bequest), and funds from the state provide the means to purchase the painting *Cardinal Muzio Gallo*, by Anton von Maron. The Alcy C. Kendrick Fund and funds from the State of North Carolina, by

exchange, enable purchase of *The Eruption of Mt. Vesuvius*, by Pierre-Jacques Volaire.[66]

In October 1982, the registration, art handling, and conservation staffs begin to move the collection from Morgan Street. Between October and December, the staff transfers approximately eight hundred paintings and sculptures. Prior to the move, over a period of several months, the conservation staff, under the direction of Chief Conservator David C. Goist, inspected, treated, and prepared for transport all of the art selected for this first phase of the move. The move is organized according to the fragility of the art and whether it will be on view for the opening of the new Museum.

4 – 5.   Spectators watch the hot
air balloons at opening festivities.

6.   Chief Designer Patrick
Sears (with paper), gives a preview of
the new building to state business leaders and public officials.

4·

5·

6.

72-73

1983 On April 5, twenty-seven years after the opening of the NCMA in 1956, Governor James B. Hunt, Jr., officially opens the new North Carolina Museum of Art. Approximately 25,000 people attend celebratory events over a two-week period.

At the opening, Governor Hunt says: "As we enjoy our splendid collection in its new setting, we need to remember the public-spirited citizens who first conceived the idea of a state art museum; the legislators who set aside funds for the collections; the businessmen and women who contributed their expertise and their money; and the visionaries who brought this building to completion."[67]

Director Bowron describes broad goals for the new museum: "Establishing the Museum in its new home, posing new standards of quality, broadening our impact on the community, and developing greater recognition."[68]

Much is "new" about the Museum. The building itself consists of approximately 180,000 square feet (compared to 45,000 square feet in the building on Morgan Street), including 50,000 square feet of exhibition space. For the first time, the Museum has its own up-to-date conservation laboratory, comparable in size and equipment to its collection. It also now has an outside conservation program to serve other museums, public galleries, state agencies, and non-profit organizations.

The Nancy Susan Reynolds Education Wing, which includes an auditorium, enables the staff to increase education programs and visitor services. The Mary Duke Biddle Gallery becomes an expanded teaching gallery for both the general public and the visually impaired. The NCMA offers, for the first time, touch tours of the regular permanent galleries — one of the first museums in the nation to offer such a program. Visually impaired persons, by special arrangement, can obtain permission to "touch" selected works.

There is a new commitment to present contemporary works of art to the broad regional audience that the NCMA serves.

The Museum announces that the

1.

2.

3.

1.   Bouguereau's *Young Girl Defending Herself against Eros* charms visitors to *French Salon Paintings from Southern Collections.*

2.   Maud Gatewood was among the North Carolina artists represented by one-person exhibitions.

3.   Museum Chief Curator William Chiego (left) and guests at the opening of the European galleries.

first triennial *North Carolina Artists Exhibition* will open in the spring of 1984.

With additional staff in the Communications, Curatorial, and Design departments, many publications are introduced to educate visitors about the new building, the collection, and programs. Director Bowron writes the first general introduction to the collection since William R. Valentiner's *Catalogue of Paintings*, published when the Museum opened in 1956.

The number and strength of the docent and volunteer organizations grows with the move to the new building and the expansion of facilities and programs. To honor the opening, the docents establish the Docent Gift Lecture Fund. Numbering more than four hundred, the

volunteers participate in the opening events and are active in several areas, helping with the information desk, hospitality, the library, Museum Shop, and education activities.

The Third Annual Southeastern Art Museum Educators' Forum takes place at the new Museum. Educators participate in sessions concerning interpretive exhibitions, audio-visual programming, and marketing programs that Educate and broaden audiences.

In June, the Museum inaugurates its special exhibitions program in the new building with *French Salon Paintings from Southern Collections*, a selection of sixty-five paintings by French artists who exhibited at the Paris Salon during the

fifty-year period of its height of popularity and influence (1848 – 1898). The High Museum of Art in Atlanta organizes the exhibition and the NCMA's chief curator, William J. Chiego, is the coordinator.

One of the first fund-raising efforts of the new Development office, simultaneous with the opening, is an annual-giving program, *Business Friends of Art*. Initially, forty-five businesses and corporations — both within and outside North Carolina — subscribe.

The grand opening in April features only a portion of the collection — the ancient, American, and twentieth-century collections. (The curators had decided to display the collections that were on view the least amount of time in the old muse-

4.

5.

um.) The staff prepares to install and open the European galleries next.

The spacious new galleries for the European collection allow the presentation, for the first time, of a continuous sequence of works, from late medieval and early Renaissance through the nineteenth century. Among the new acquisitions first exhibited is a pair of Italian mythological paintings — *Mercury Lulling Argus to Sleep* and *Mercury About to Behead Argus*, by Ubaldo Gandolfi. The Art Society donates funds from the Phifer Bequest for the acquisition of the two paintings in memory of Robert Lee Humber. Art Society Phifer funds — along with state funds — also allow the Museum to purchase the French nineteenth-century painting *Portrait of Madame Carolus-Duran*, by Carolus-Duran (Charles-Emile-August Durand), to honor Zöe Strawn Webster. Webster was executive secretary of the Art Society for fifteen years before her retirement in 1983. A major contribution from Dr. Abram Kanof and Dr. Frances Pascher Kanof funds construction of the Judaic Gallery. Prior to the gallery's December opening, the curators consulted Kanof about the installation and preparation of a gallery guide. Since 1975, Kanof had been helping to develop a collection of Jewish ceremonial art, and the Kanofs give a sixteenth-century German silver relief, *David Dancing Before the Ark of the Covenant*, for the gallery's opening.

1984 *The North Carolina Artists Exhibition 1984*, selected by guest curator Howard Fox, opens in April and includes 109 works in a variety of media and techniques, including painting, sculpture, photography, film, video, weaving, ceramics, metalwork, jewelry, and site-specific installations. There are a record number of entries: 1,466 works by 812 artists. Huston Paschal, assistant curator, organizes the exhibition and also edits the first fully illustrated *NCAE* catalogue.

Other exhibitions opening during the first full calendar year in the new building offer wide diversity. *Howard Pyle and the Wyeths: Four Generations of American Imagination* is the Museum's most popular exhibition to date. It includes sixty-one paintings, drawings, and books that reflect Pyle's influence on three generations of the Wyeth family — N. C., Andrew, and Jamie Wyeth. Coordinated by Chief Curator William J. Chiego, the exhibition also includes additional private loans from North Carolina collectors. Hudson-Belk and Central Carolina Bank provide generous support for the exhibition.

The exhibition *Baroque Paintings from the Bob Jones University Collection*, the major loan exhibition for the summer, includes forty-four Italian, Dutch, Flemish, French, and Spanish paintings of the seventeenth and eighteenth centuries. This exhibition of works from the South Carolina university's collection of sacred art is its first presentation outside the university. David Steel, associate curator of European art, organizes the show and writes the fully illustrated catalogue that accompanies the exhibition.

In the fall of 1984, the exhibition *American Art Since 1970: Painting, Sculpture and Drawings from the Collection of the Whitney Museum of American Art* opens. This selection of forty-five works, from the collection generally considered to be the finest of its kind, includes works which focus on the social concerns of contemporary artists. Mitchell Kahan, curator of American and contemporary art, coordinates the exhibition, and members of the Business Friends of Art group and the NCMA Foundation help sponsor the Raleigh show.

1–4.   Scenes from 1984 exhibitions: (1) the *North Carolina Artists Exhibition* with installation in progress, (2) Head Exhibition Designer Patrick Sears (left) and Associate Director Gay Hertzman (center) at *Howard Pyle and the Wyeths*, (3) *American Art since 1970*, and (4) *Jugtown*, which featured traditional North Carolina pottery.

5.   The Madeleine Johnson Heidrick Bequest provides funds for the purchase of contemporary works such as *Cabbage Worship* by British artists Gilbert and George.

      Previous pages: The public opening in April, 1983.

CABBAGE
WORSHIP
Gilbert AND George
1982

78–79

Eleven other special exhibitions open this year. *Gilbert and George/Richard Long*, organized by Mitchell Kahan, celebrates the four-hundredth anniversary of British settlement in North Carolina. Also presented are two exhibitions from the permanent collection, *Jugtown Pottery: The Busbee Vision*, organized by Assistant Director Gay M. Hertzman, and *Works on Paper by North Carolina Artists*, organized by Huston Paschal.

With funds provided by the Art Society (Phifer Bequest), the Museum acquires a life-size Roman marble statue, *Emperor Caracalla in the Guise of Helios*. The Madeleine Johnson Heidrick Bequest (restricted to the acquisition of contemporary works of art) provides funds for the

acquisition of *American Landscapes with Revolutionary Heroes*, by Roger Brown, and *Cabbage Worship*, by British artists Gilbert and George.

The curatorial staff, in association with other scholars, begins to assess the collection to determine its strengths and weaknesses. Director Bowron and the curators determine that some works are of inferior quality or condition, duplicative of other works in the collection, or otherwise inappropriate and recommend to the board of trustees that the works be deaccessioned. Most of these works, acquired largely by gifts over the years, are in the ancient, African, New World, and European decorative arts collections. Plans are made to acquire other works of

art using the funds received from the sale of the deaccessioned works.

1.

1985 The major exhibition for the summer is *Art Nouveau to Art Moderne: Twentieth-Century Decorative Arts from the Metropolitan Museum of Art*. The exhibition is organized by the Walters Art Gallery in Baltimore, where it opens before traveling to the NCMA. Coordinating curator in Raleigh is William J. Chiego.

At the June meeting of the board of trustees, Director Bowron announces his resignation, effective September 1985, to become director of the Harvard University Art Museums.

The General Assembly reduces the budget by approximately $230,000, about 10 percent. The most serious impact is the loss of several security positions, forcing the Museum to close on Tuesdays as well as Mondays. The General Assembly also discontinues the allocation of state purchase funds for works of art.[69]

In July, the Museum and its conservation staff sponsor a refresher course on the theory and practice of cleaning and restoring paintings. Conservators from museums, regional centers, and private practices in the United States and Canada attend. The North Carolina State University Visual Arts Center in Raleigh co-hosts the course.

Leaks have been a major problem since the new building's completion. In September, the state Department of Administration assumes full responsibility for repairs to the roof. Ultimately, repairs stop the most serious leaks in the European galleries and art storage areas.

Following the departure of Edgar Peters Bowron in September, the board asks Gay Mahaffy Hertzman, associate director, to serve as acting director. (Hertzman was previously acting director for eight months prior to Bowron's appointment in May 1981.)

In October, Patric Dorsey, secretary of the Department of Cultural Resources, names Richard S. Schneiderman director. Schneiderman, director of the Georgia Museum of Art at the University of Georgia, will take office at the NCMA in May 1986. He earned his Ph.D. from the State University of New York at Binghamton and was formerly curator of prints and drawings at the Georgia Museum of Art.

1.	Leaks, a problem since the building's completion, were repaired during 1985.

2.	Diana Suarez Phillips, coordinator of youth programs, demonstrates a primitive motion picture machine to Dr. James Semans in *Of Space and Time*.

2.

During 1985, the governor's Efficiency Study Commission recommends state funding for the Museum be phased out over five years and that it become a private institution. In December the Museum Board of Directors, under the leadership of Chairman Gordon Hanes, recommends to the governor that the NCMA remain a state museum belonging to the people of North Carolina. Governor James G. Martin (1985 – 1993) announces that he will not ask the legislature to act on the commission's recommendation.

The Mary Duke Biddle Gallery opens the third of its annual exhibitions, *Of Space and Time: Motion in Art*, in October. Organized by the Museum's coordinator of youth programs, Diana Suarez, the exhibition receives major support from the Mary Duke Biddle Foundation, with additional funding provided by Ralph and Janie P. Price.

In November, twenty-five pieces of ancient glass from the permanent collection are on view. The installation includes Egyptian, Roman, and Islamic pieces dating from the sixth century B. C. through the tenth century A. D. Mary Ellen Soles, curator of ancient art, organizes the exhibition.

THE MUSEUM IN TRANSITION, 1986–1990

"That the development has been so steady and has reached such heights is in large part a result of the dynamic relationship of the various groups that have, at different times and in varying degrees, played decisive roles in shaping the institution."

—Gay Mahaffy Hertzman, Museum Associate Director, 1981–90

1986 As the North Carolina Museum of Art celebrates its thirtieth anniversary, it also enters a period of transition.

Richard S. Schneiderman assumes the position of director in May. One of his first priorities is to plan a budget for fiscal year 1986 – 87 which includes an appropriation increase from the General Assembly for new statewide Museum programs. The legislature approves the request and increases the 1986 – 87 appropriation by $250,000 (almost the same amount as the 1985 reduction). The increase enables the Museum to fund four new staff positions and introduce statewide outreach programs. Gordon Hanes, chairman of the board of trustees, states that "the philosophy of the program is to reach new audiences — the 'non visitor' — and . . . to encourage the enjoyment, appreciation, and study of art."[70]

Guided tours are given to 37,000 visitors during the fiscal year, among the highest totals of all American art museums and near the top among southeastern art museums. Much of the success of the program is due to the docents, who lead more than 3,000 tours.

The continuing generosity of Gordon and Copey Hanes is particularly significant during 1986. Altogether they donate nineteen works to the Museum — notably adding to the ancient, African, Oceanic, and New World collections. Their gifts include a Cycladic *Female Figurine*, a Roman *Torso of an Emperor in the Guise of Jupiter*, and a Vera Cruz *Priestess*.

Special exhibitions complement the old master collection and introduce the work of contemporary artists. *Dutch Art in the Age of Rembrandt* includes forty-five works from the Museum's collection of seventeenth-century Dutch art. The exhibition also includes a selection of etchings by Rembrandt — borrowed from public and private collections — and a group of original copper plates for the etchings. The copper plates, on view as a group for the first time in thirty years, are from the estate of Robert Lee Humber. David Steel, associate curator of European art, organizes the exhibition and coordinates the symposium that attracts many leading scholars of Dutch art.

2.

3.

1.

4.

1.   *Dutch Art in the Age of Rembrandt* included 45 works, some of which had been among the earliest to enter the permanent collection.

2.   *Methods of the Masters* focused on the variety of techniques and materials used by artists over the centuries.

3.   A mask from Nigeria in the form of a sawfish fascinates school-children in the African Galleries.

4.   Win Utermohlen, Design Department signage technician, gives a children's workshop in screenprinting for the Education Department.

The Public Art Show is a group exhibition featuring the art of approximately thirty contemporary artists working in a variety of formats. Some works are commentaries on public issues, especially the influence of the media. Mitchell D. Kahan, curator of American and contemporary art, coordinates the exhibition, organized for the Nexus Contemporary Art Center, Atlanta. Funding by the NEA and the North Carolina Museum of Art Foundation supports the exhibition.

In late 1986, the Museum opens *Methods of the Masters: Techniques in Art*, a didactic exhibition in the Mary Duke Biddle Gallery that focuses on artists' techniques over the centuries, such as egg tempera painting on panel, painting on canvas, stone carving, and bronze casting. Support for the exhibition comes from funds provided by the Z. Smith Reynolds Foundation and the Mary Duke Biddle Foundation. Diana Suarez, coordinator of youth programs, is exhibition organizer.

The first of a planned series of catalogues pertaining to various NCMA collections is published. *The Catalogue of Spanish Paintings* presents research on the Museum's thirty-four Spanish paintings and includes a number of new attributions. Professor Edward J. Sullivan of New York University writes the catalogue, and a grant from the Andrew W. Mellon Foundation supports its research. Grants from the NEA and the North Carolina Museum of Art Foundation fund the catalogue's publication.

Chief Curator William J. Chiego resigns to become director of the Allen Memorial Art Museum, Oberlin College, Oberlin, Ohio. Mitchell D. Kahan, curator of American and contemporary art, resigns to become director of the Akron Art Museum, Akron, Ohio.

The board of trustees, with the support and concurrence of the Art Society Board of Directors and the North Carolina Museum of Art Foundation, requests a plan to strengthen and define Museum growth, addressing landscape needs, site use planning, and capital requirements. The director and staff respond with a proposal that eventually becomes the basis for the *Art + Landscape* master plan for

the Museum building and site.

The Museum's new director Richard Schneiderman and NCMA Board of Trustees Chairman Gordon Hanes ask Art Society President Anne Boyer to appoint an ad hoc committee, composed of the five most recent past society presidents, to study membership office activities and responsibilities. The committee recommends transferring membership responsibilities, including managing income from dues, to the Museum development staff. The Art Society retains management of the Phifer Bequest fund and other restricted funds and continues to advise the staff on membership issues.

1987 The new year begins by celebrating the opening of the African, Oceanic, and New World galleries, the last major areas of the collection to be installed. Grants from the James G. Hanes and Anna H. Hanes Foundations provide funding to complete gallery construction and install works of art. On Sunday, January 10, following the opening of the new galleries, 3,849 people visit the Museum — a record for a single day. Allen Wardwell, director of the Noguchi Museum in New York and consultative curator for this project, selected approximately one hundred objects for permanent display. Mary Ellen Soles, curator of ancient art, coordinated the gallery installations.

In February, Susan J. Barnes succeeds

William J. Chiego as chief curator. A former associate curator for exhibitions at Rice University Museum, Barnes was assistant dean of the Center for Advanced Study in the Visual Arts at the National Gallery of Art before coming to the NCMA.

Two American nineteenth-century paintings are acquired during the year. Art Society funds (Phifer Bequest) and funds from various donors, by exchange, provide for the purchase of *Bridal Veil Falls, Yosemite*, by Albert Bierstadt. The Museum acquires the painting *Salt Marsh at Southport, Connecticut*, by Martin Johnson Heade, with funds from the sale of deaccessioned works of art.

The review of the collection contin-

ues with a focus on prints, as recommended by Director Schneiderman, an active scholar in the field. Print collecting, never pursued in a deliberate, systematic way at the Museum, has resulted in a group of sporadically acquired works of uneven quality. Scholarly review indicates that European and American prints made before 1900 should be deaccessioned.

The curatorial staff, in collaboration with other departments, organizes fourteen exhibitions for the Museum's four changing exhibition spaces. *Sir David Wilkie of Scotland*, the first North American exhibition devoted to the work of this important British artist of the Romantic era, premieres at the Yale Center for British Art before traveling to Raleigh. The

NCMA's former chief curator, William J. Chiego, organizes the exhibition and leads the team of British and American scholars who produce the catalogue.

The North Carolina Artists Exhibition, now a triennial, opens in July and contains 110 works by 35 artists. The guest curator, *New York Times* art critic Roberta Smith, reviewed slides submitted by 628 artists and traveled around the state to make studio visits prior to selecting the works for exhibition.

The exhibition *The Arts at Black Mountain College* commemorates the thirtieth anniversary of the college's closing in 1956. Bard College, Annandale-on-Hudson, New York, organizes the exhibition with Mary Emma Harris, guest

curator. Harris, author of the catalogue, was also the chief researcher of the Black Mountain College project at the NCMA in 1973. Assistant Curator Huston Paschal, who worked on the Black Mountain project with Harris, coordinates the exhibition in Raleigh. The exhibition received support from the NEA, which also had contributed to the Museum's research project in the 1970s.

The family of Gordon Hanes makes a substantial contribution to the Museum in 1987, to honor Hanes on his seventieth birthday. The John and Mary Camp Foundation is one of the first contributors to the Robert Lee Humber Lecture Fund.

The NCMA receives two grants from the NEA: $50,000 in support of the exhibi-

2. Design staff members Kerry Boyd and Rich Goldberg assemble the complex installation for the kimono displays.

3 – 5. *Robes of Elegance* set new attendance records for the Museum.

2.

3.

1.

1. Director Richard Schneiderman (second from left) meets with trustees, the design team, and staff to discuss *Art + Landscape*.

tion *Sir David Wilkie of Scotland*, and an advance gift of $20,000 to assist in organizing and presenting the exhibition *Robes of Elegance*, scheduled for the spring of 1988. BB&T is a leading corporate contributor in 1987. Northern Telecom provides monetary and exceptional in-kind assistance with the loan of several managerial personnel to help with membership recruitment and corporate solicitations.

With the support of the North Carolina Museum of Art Foundation, Samuel M. Stone III, director of development, expands the department to include new staff to promote growth and improve membership, accounting, and computer operations.

The NCMA receives awards and recognition from the American Association of Museums and the Art Museum Association for the design of several of its publications and printed materials.

During the year, the boards and staff meet to discuss a long-range master plan for the Museum and surrounding area. Head Designer Lida M. Lowry suggests including landscape architects and visual artists in the planning process. The NEA awards the Museum a grant that enables a nationwide search for an inter-disciplinary team to carry out the project design. Subsequently, visual artists, architects, landscape architects, planners, and designers throughout the country are invited to form teams and submit their

qualifications for review. More than ninety responses are received by September.

In December, a distinguished panel of experts in contemporary public art, museum education, landscape architecture, and inter-disciplinary design collaboration unanimously recommend a design team from New York to produce a proposal for the master plan. The team combines an internationally known visual artist, Barbara Kruger, with two architects, Henry Smith-Miller and Laurie Hawkinson, who have varied experiences in architecture, product design, and exhibition design. Landscape architect Nicholas Quenell, experienced in large-scale environmental planning, completes the team.

The Museum appoints Patricia Fuller,

4.

"Brought here for you are not only creations, but originals from the hands of artists and craftsmen from many times and places — the great creators on canvas, paper, in wood, marble, bronze and precious metals. To fully realize our good fortune will take many visits and growing knowledge — but you will be well repaid."
— *Joseph C. Sloane*

5.

formerly coordinator of the NEA program "Art in Public Places," as project consultant.

The Museum embarks on a ten-year project to create and implement a site plan for the 140 acres of state land that surround the building. The State of North Carolina begins a review of all state property bordering Blue Ridge Road.

The 1987 session of the General Assembly funds eleven security positions and one full-time assistant conservator position. Legislators also approve a bill, introduced by state senators Tony Rand and Aaron Plyler, appropriating $475,000 for remedial work on the building and grounds.

1988 In January, the NCMA receives the one-millionth visitor to the new building.

The newly selected design team begins working at the Museum in February as an integral part of the site-planning process, meeting with the director and staff members to assess needs and gather information for the *Art + Landscape* plan.

In March, the Museum celebrates another milestone — its three millionth visitor since opening on Morgan Street in 1956. Fewer than two million people visited during the twenty-seven years it was in its former location; more than one million have visited the new building in only five years. The increase in visitor attendance is attributed to expanded facilities

that show more of the art collection and present more educational programs and exhibitions.

Also in March, the exhibition *Robes of Elegance: Japanese Kimonos of the Sixteenth through Twentieth Centuries* sets new attendance records for the average number of visitors per day, 865; and for the total number of visitors to an exhibition, 70,039. To prevent crowding on weekends, the Museum institutes a free pass system for visitors. The exhibition, conceived and organized by Director Richard Schneiderman and coordinated by Susan Barnes, chief curator, traces the artistic development of the kimono in three successive installations of thirty kimonos each, displayed chronologically.

The art objects from Japan are the first direct loans from that country to an institution in the South. It is also the first time the Museum has received indemnification from the Federal Council on the Arts and the Humanities through the NEA's Museum Program. In addition to NEA support, generous funding is provided by the Broyhill Family Foundation, Hudson Belk and Belk-Leggett Companies, and Mitsubishi Semiconductor Electric America.

The Art Society donates funds from the Phifer Bequest to enable the Museum to acquire a steel and aluminum sculpture, *Three Elements*, by Canadian-American artist Ronald Bladen. The sculpture is dedicated to Gordon and Copey Hanes.

A Roman *Sarcophagus (Osteotheke)*, used for burials during the second century A. D., adds to the classical collection — a gift from Anne and Carl Carlson, in memory of Lynn and Karl Prickett.

Funds provided by the 1986 legislature have enabled the NCMA to expand art education and exhibition services throughout the state. In 1988, the Museum employs a lecturer for special audiences and a public programs coordinator, who work with art councils, galleries, libraries, schools, senior citizen groups, civic clubs, social service agencies, and other groups in North Carolina communities. The Museum also provides a limited number of traveling exhibitions, building on the foundation established in previous

years by the Art Society.

In August 1988, a pilot program, *Movies on the Lawn: Back to the Drive-in*, draws an average of 450 people for each film. The family festival event in April, *A Celebration of Japan*, draws 4,575 visitors, setting a new attendance record for the program.

An expanded Development Department, together with the staff and the NCMA Foundation, begins to focus on corporate and foundation fund-raising. Membership in the Museum and in the Business Friends of Art group increases by 50 percent during the fiscal year.

The Art of Irregardless, directed by J. Arthur Gordon, assumes responsibility for food service in the Café.

3.

4.

1.	Director Schneiderman (center) and the *Art + Landscape* design team tour the Museum grounds.

2.	Henry Smith-Miller, an *Art + Landscape* design team member, explains an NCMA site model at a public forum.

3.	Gordon Hanes at the dedication of the sculpture *Three Elements* in his and Copey Hanes's honor.

4.	Ronald Bladen's *Three Elements* was the first work installed on Museum grounds as part of the *Art + Landscape* plan.

5.	Casual crowds flock to the *Movies on the Lawn* series.

5.

88–89

The General Assembly in 1988 appropriates an additional $474,000 for continuing remedial work to improve the Museum grounds and building.

The NEA approves, under the new Challenge III grant program, a potential grant of $250,000 for the *Art + Landscape* plan. To receive the grant, the Museum must first raise $750,000.

Early in the year the staff, along with the *Art + Landscape* design team, receives a variety of ideas from the community for ways to use the Museum site. The design team meets with the board of trustees and staff, state government representatives, local botanists, and others in the community. In October 1988, the team presents an initial proposal to the full board, and the trustees unanimously recommend plan approval to the General Assembly and other state government agencies.

By the end of the year, all three of the Museum's governing bodies meet to discuss plans to launch a capital campaign. A temporary steering committee is appointed, consisting of members from each of the three governing boards.

1. *Objects of Bright Pride* featured works created by Native Americans of the Northwest.

2. Works by artists Arliss Watford (left) and Clyde Jones (seated on one of his *Critters*) appeared in *Signs and Wonders: Outsider Art Inside North Carolina.*

3. James Harold Jennings made his own headdress for the opening of *Signs and Wonders*.

1989 Susan J. Barnes, chief curator since 1987, resigns in January to become senior curator of Western art at the Dallas Museum of Art.

In March, the first work installed on the grounds as a part of the *Art + Landscape* plan is the tall rectangular sculpture *Three Elements*, by Ronald Bladen, purchased in 1988.

Exhibitions this year include art from two major American museums: *Objects of Bright Pride: Northwest Coast Indian Art from the American Museum of Natural History* and *Immaterial Objects: Works from the Permanent Collection of the Whitney Museum of American Art*. Other exhibitions also focus on American art and contemporary North Carolina artists.

Since opening the new building in 1983, more than a dozen exhibitions featuring the work of North Carolinians, including Maud Gatewood, Russ Warren, Minnie Evans, Vernon Pratt, and Clarence Morgan, have been organized.

The Museum organizes *Signs and Wonders: Outsider Art Inside North Carolina*, featuring the works of North Carolina self-taught artists. Guest curator Roger Manly and Curator of European Art David Steel organize the exhibition, and the NEA provides partial support.

Anthony F. Janson becomes the chief curator in September 1989. Janson, a specialist in European painting, has held senior curatorial positions at the Indianapolis Museum of Art and the Ringling

Museum of Art in Sarasota, Florida.

Throughout the year, the Museum expands and improves its statewide outreach programs. These programs support and assist schools, art groups, correctional and psychiatric institutions, and other audiences with special needs. An outreach program is also initiated, allowing volunteers across the state to present slide programs based on the permanent collection and special exhibitions.

The Museum board of trustees, the Museum Foundation, the Art Society, and the staff begin to formulate plans for a capital campaign. The Development staff together with members of the three governing boards, plans to launch the campaign the following year.

In the image: BAD GIRL GOS TO HELL AND BEATS HELL OUT OF THE DEVIL

1990 Along with all other state agencies, the Museum confronts a 4.5 percent reduction in state government funding, due to a projected budget shortfall. Some of the effects of the shortfall are offset with revenue from continuing membership growth and funds from several corporations that agree to sponsor planned exhibitions. NEA grants also benefit the Museum during this time.

The Capital Area Planning Commission and the Department of Administration approve and endorse the *Art + Landscape* master plan, which the state subsequently incorporates into its plan for the Blue Ridge Road corridor. The endorsement encourages the Museum's three boards and the Development office,

under the leadership of William Anlyan, Jr., to move forward with the capital campaign to raise funds for the *Art + Landscape* project.

Director Schneiderman and the senior staff begin long-term planning and evaluation of exhibitions, publications, and programs. At the same time, the curatorial staff, under the direction of Anthony Janson, reviews the permanent collection to determine its present status and plan future growth. The curatorial plan includes an important change in direction: a new emphasis on building a strong modern art collection.

Purchases and gifts during 1990 reflect the philosophy of the curatorial plan. The large bronze sculpture *Untitled*,

by American artist Joel Shapiro, is the most important contemporary work to enter the collection in nearly a decade. The contemporary painting *Reflections*, by New York artist Martha Diamond, is acquired with funds from the NEA, the Deal Foundation, and the Art Society (Phifer Bequest).

Another purchase with funds from the Art Society is *Untitled*, by Moshe Kupferman, Israel's leading painter. This acquisition marks the beginning of an effort to broaden the scope of the modern collection to include works by foreign artists, thereby presenting a more balanced survey of contemporary art.

An important addition to the ancient art collection, purchased with funds pro-

"Upon being told that the Museum's collection contained no modern art and that the Art Commission purchased no modern art, [Valentiner] said, 'We will borrow some. We will open a museum in totality . . . . People who are not attentive to the art of their own time can not justly appreciate the art of the past.' "
— *Benjamin F. Williams*

3.

vided by the Art Society, is a fifth-century B. C. Greek vase, *Neck Amphora*, attributed to the Three Line Group.

Although the NCMA's permanent collection is the center of its artistic program, special exhibitions complement and extend its mission. During 1990, the Museum's special exhibition program receives support from the corporate community and private contributions. *An American Collection: Paintings and Sculpture from the National Academy of Design*, coordinated by John Coffey, curator of American and modern art since 1988, receives support from Northern Telecom. *Making Faces: Self-Portraits by Alex Katz*, which Coffey also organizes, is one of the few exhibitions that is organized for trav-

el to another state. Burroughs Wellcome Company contributes funds for the exhibition.

North Carolina Artists Exhibition 1990, selected by Guest Curator Stephen Westfall and coordinated by Associate Curator of Modern Art Huston Paschal and Assistant Curator Christine Jones Huber, receives generous support from Wachovia Bank. *Man and Myth in Classical Greece: Red-Figure Attic Vases from the Walters Art Gallery*, organized by Mary Ellen Soles, curator of ancient art, complements the Museum's own collection of ancient vases. It receives support from contributions administered by the North Carolina Museum of Art Foundation.

Under the leadership of Ron Doggett,

chairman and chief executive officer of Goodmark Foods, Business Friends of Art remains a strong supporter of the Museum, as does the Business Friends Council.

The Contemporaries, a newly organized group for young adult members begins to initiate fund-raising events such as the *Rock and Roll Lawn Party*, the *New Year's Eve Extravaganza*, and the *Nouveau Beaujolais Wine Tasting*.

Glaxo Inc. pledges $250,000 to support the exhibition *Nature into Art: English Landscape Watercolors from the British Museum*, scheduled to open in 1991. Glaxo's pledge is the largest the NCMA has yet received to support a single exhibition.

With funds provided by the Samuel

5.

6.

7.

3.   Installing Joel Shapiro's sculpture *Untitled* required great precision.

4 – 5.   The Contemporaries, a group organized in 1990 for young adult members, initiated events such as the *New Year's Eve Extravaganza* (4), and *Rock and Roll Lawn Party* (5).

6.   Associate Director Gay Hertzman and staff members admire the plans for a garden area on Museum grounds to be created with funds given in honor of her retirement.

7.   Visitors encounter the many sides of the artist in *Making Faces: Self-Portraits by Alex Katz.*

H. Kress Foundation and the Newington-Cropsey Foundation, the Museum revives the *Bulletin*, its scholarly journal about the collection. The issue published in 1990, after a ten-year hiatus, features ancient art in the Museum's collection.

The Education Department, under the leadership of Joseph Covington, reports that 1990 participation in the Museum's education programs reached its highest level ever, with more than 45,000 people attending. The number of family festivals increases from two to three; these festivals attract more participants than any other single-event programs.

Gay M. Hertzman, associate director, retires at the end of 1990, after a twenty-three year career at the Museum. She held a number of curatorial positions before being appointed chief curator in 1980. Hertzman became associate director in 1981 and was acting director twice, first in 1980 and again in 1985.

SETTING LONG-RANGE GOALS, 1991 – 1993

"We chaired the campaign for the Park Theater — what a unique project for a Museum. It never could have happened unless we had moved to the 'new' North Carolina Museum of Art!"

—*Mazie Froelich, President of the Art Society, 1981–82, and member of the Museum Board of Trustees*

1991 Early in the year Heyward H. McKinney, Jr. becomes associate director. McKinney was formerly assistant secretary for administrative services in the Department of Cultural Resources and has worked closely with the Museum since 1985.

The board of trustees accepts the long-range planning document for the Museum's artistic mission, which Director Schneiderman and the senior staff have been developing since 1990. The plan calls for a renewed emphasis on the permanent collection — rehanging and reinstalling works of art where necessary, providing new and better instructive wall labels and signage, and reassessing the objects in storage. In addition, the plan includes a commitment to acquire contemporary art as one of its primary goals. The long-range plan also recommends reducing the number of special exhibitions, which have been a drain on staff and resources, while increasing the quality and educational scope of these shows. The long-range planning document also focuses attention on extending services to North Carolina's minorities.

The NCMA is fortunate to receive several important gifts that echo its efforts to implement the long-range plan. Gifts from Gordon and Copey Hanes supplement the Greek, Egyptian, and African collections.[71] An anonymous gift of a painting by German artist Hans Thoma, *Miraculous Birds*, helps to fill a gap in the late nineteenth-century European collection. The Museum also acquires, as a bequest from Nell Hirschberg, *Standing Woman Combing Hair*, by Alexander Archipenko — a complement to the larger Archipenko sculpture *Blue Dancer*, purchased in 1976. This year's purchases include the French neoclassical painting *The Death of Alcestis*, by Pierre Peyron, and *Landscape in Ecuador*, by American landscape painter Louis Rémy Mignot.

During the year, the Museum also purchases paintings by three American twentieth-century artists. *Six Women*, by Alex Katz, is one of the artist's most ambitious compositions and his largest single canvas. *Double Dare*, by North Carolina native William T. Williams, is made possi-

1. *Objects of Delight* in the Mary Duke Biddle Gallery included still-life paintings from the permanent collection.

"It would be so valuable if every member would indicate to his or her friends and to people they meet the importance of supporting this Museum — the benefits, both tangible and intangible, that come from membership. To know that this state owns such an institution should bring pride to every North Carolinian."
— Ann Turner, President of the Art Society, 1980–81, former member of the board of trustees, and member of the NCMA Foundation.

ble by funds from the Art Society (Phifer Bequest). Funds from Thomas S. Kenan III and the NEA allow the purchase of the landscape *Three Trees, Two Clouds*, by North Carolina native John Beerman. The purchase of the work by Beerman, who is pursuing a successful career in New York, reaffirms the Museum's interest in North Carolina artists, especially those who have achieved national recognition.

Although fewer in number, the exhibitions shown during the year reflect the Museum's commitment to quality, scope, and educational potential. *Nature into Art: Landscape Watercolors from the British Museum*, coordinated by Director Schneiderman, is the third most popular exhibition to date. The Mary Duke Biddle

Education Gallery displays *Objects of Delight: Three Hundred Years of Still-Life Painting*. The exhibition, organized by Anthony Janson, chief curator, and Joseph Covington, director of the Education Department, displays European and American still lifes from the permanent collection. Also shown in 1991 is an exhibition of the work of Israeli artist Moshe Kupferman. Organized by John Coffey, the exhibition is the first major show of the artist's work in the United States and the genesis for the Israel/North Carolina Cultural Exchange program in 1996 – 97.

Consistent with an emphasis on the permanent collection, the curatorial and design staffs redesign the galleries on the entrance level to provide more open, con-

tiguous spaces. The newly renovated space also provides a special exhibition gallery.

In October, Burroughs Wellcome makes a $250,000 gift to the Museum for the *Art + Landscape* project.[72] Currently, the company is lending the Museum a major work by contemporary artist Jennifer Bartlett from its own corporate art collection.

Mazie and Jake Froelich, chairpersons of the Capital Campaign Steering Committee, and the other members of that committee successfully meet the first requirement of the NEA challenge grant. Subsequently, the NEA awards the first part of the grant, $150,000, for the *Art + Landscape* project.

1.

With this positive step, Daniel P. Gottlieb, the Museum's newly appointed chief designer, together with the director and staff, begins to work with the design team to develop the first phase of the *Art + Landscape* project — the construction of an amphitheater adjacent to the south facade of the building.

The Museum continues to receive support from the Kress Foundation for curatorial and conservation research on the collection. The Kress Foundation donates $30,000 to publish a catalogue of the Italian painting collection. These funds, together with a $30,000 grant from the NEA, are to support project research and sponsor the catalogue.

1992 Early in the year, *The Age of the Marvelous* opens. Organized by the Hood Museum of Art at Dartmouth College, the exhibition complements the NCMA collection of sixteenth-and seventeenth-century art and includes more than seven hundred objects of all types: paintings, prints, microscopes, books, sea shells, and stuffed animals and birds. Coordinated by Chief Curator Anthony Janson, *The Age of the Marvelous* averages 734 visitors a day.

Another exhibition, *But the Ball is Lost and the Mallet Slipped*, opens late in 1991 and continues until February 1992. An installation piece by the contemporary Irish-born artist Michael Timpson, the exhibition intermingles substance and speculation in a walk-through installa-

tion. Huston Paschal organizes the exhibition and writes the catalogue.

Funds provided by IBM enable the opening of a timely exhibition in March 1992. *From the Ground Up: Experiencing Architecture* includes a model of the Museum and a hands-on computer-aided design system to encourage visitors to learn about effective architecture. Diana Suarez Phillips, staff coordinator of youth programs, and Georgia Bizios, professor of architecture at North Carolina State University, organize the exhibition.

The State Building Commission unanimously endorses the New York team of Smith-Miller, Hawkinson, Quenell, and Kruger as designers of the new amphitheater.

2.
3.

4.

The Age of the Marvelous evoked the amazing conglomerations amassed by collectors during the Renaissance and Baroque periods.

From the Ground Up explored the plans and building methods used in the construction of the museum building.

J. Carter Brown, Director of the National Gallery of Art in Washington, D. C. views Joseph Cornell's *Suzy's Sun (for Judy Tyler)* while at the NCMA for the meeting of the Association of Art Museum Directors.

Artist Michael Timpson (left), assisted by Tom Lopez, head production technician, installs his exhibition *But the Ball is Lost and the Mallet Chipped.*

Director Schneiderman assumes leadership of the Capital Campaign, after the resignation of William Anlyan, associate director of development. The kick-off begins in June 1992. The immediate campaign goal is to raise additional money before the deadline set by the NEA Challenge III grant. To aid this effort, the Museum employs Anne Jones, a specialist in recruiting finance and accounting professionals for business and industry, to head the Development Department.

Also in June, the NCMA hosts some ninety museum directors from all parts of the United States for the annual meeting of the Association of Art Museum Directors. The Ackland Art Museum is co-host for the event.

Funds from the Art Society, Phifer Bequest, and the State of North Carolina, by exchange, enable the purchase of an American Colonial portrait painting by John Singleton Copley, *Mrs. James Russell.* The society also funds the acquisition of an Italian marble neoclassical sculpture, *Venus Italica,* from the studio of Antonio Canova. *Pigeon,* an oil on canvas on laminated wood construction by Elizabeth Murray, is purchased with funds from the sale of deaccessioned works of art. Received as gifts are a group of ancient Roman glass objects and several preparatory drawings and sketches by contemporary American artists.

A group of twenty-five Roman glass objects, first through third century A. D., a

gift by Elizabeth F. Gervais-Gruen, complements the collection of ancient glass. Artist John Beerman donates a lithograph study for his painting *Three Trees, Two Clouds,* purchased in 1991. Alex Katz gives three oil sketches and thirty-one ballpoint pen sketches on paper, all studies for his painting *Six Women.* Michael Timpson contributes two drawings made for his installation piece exhibited at the Museum in 1991–92.

The General Assembly appropriates $486,000 to complete repair work on the building's exterior masonry.

The Museum receives a $50,000 gift from an anonymous donor to establish the Dr. Abram Kanof Family Day Festival.[73]

1993 Acquisitions and exhibitions during continue to reflect the Museum's long-range goals. One of the most significant old master paintings acquired in some years is *Meat Stall with the Holy Family Giving Alms*, by the Netherlandish artist Pieter Aertsen. The painting is an early example of the type of work known as a market-piece, a combination of still-life and genre subjects. Funds from Wendell and Linda Murphy and various donors enable the purchase of the painting.

For its twentieth-century collection of non-American paintings, the Museum purchases *People on Fire*, by the Argentinean artist Guillermo Kuitca. The painting is the Museum's first work of contemporary Latin American art.

The NCMA continues to organize international exhibitions to extend its own collection. The exhibition *Naked Soul: Polish Fin-de-Siècle Painting from the National Museum, Poznan*, includes forty-six paintings, most of which are on view for the first time in the United States; many received restoration treatment especially for this exhibition.[74] Director Richard Schneiderman organizes the exhibition; the coordinator is Anthony Janson, chief curator. The Museum receives grants for the exhibition and catalogue from the Kathleen Price and Joseph M. Bryan Family Foundation and the Kosciuszko Foundation, with additional support from Delta Air Lines, Branch Banking and Trust Company, First Union Bank, the Mary Duke Biddle Foundation, IBM, and SAS Institute. The Museum receives indemnification for the exhibition from the Federal Council on the Art and the Humanities.

Yoruba Art: A Living Tradition opens in the Mary Duke Biddle Gallery in late 1993 and remains on view until June 1994. The exhibition focuses on four Yoruba objects in the Museum's collection and includes twenty-nine objects borrowed from both public and private collections, primarily in North Carolina. Rebecca Martin Nagy, associate director of Education, organizes the exhibition for the Museum, assisted by Gaynell Bowles, coordinator of adult programs.

In the autumn of 1993, the NCMA

hosts the annual meeting of the Museum Trustee Association; Ann Turner serves as chairwoman. Nearly two hundred trustees from across the United States and Canada attend. Turner, former Art Society president, Museum trustee, and current foundation board member, organizes the event.

The North Carolina Museum of Art receives national attention in October when the United States Postal Service holds a First Day of Issue ceremony at the Museum for the 1993 traditional Christmas stamp. The stamp depicts a painting from the Museum's collection, *Madonna and Child in a Landscape*, by Giovanni Battista Cima da Conegliano. The NCMA is only the third museum to receive the dis-

tinction of having a painting selected for a Christmas stamp, joining the ranks of the National Gallery of Art and the Museum of Fine Arts, Houston. The Postal Service estimates it sold 950 million stamps depicting this painting during the 1993 holiday season.

Several major staff changes take place this year. Director Richard Schneiderman resigns. Department of Cultural Resources Secretary Betty Ray McCain states that "the differences between Schneiderman and some members of the Museum's boards and of the staff were too great to be resolved."[75] Anthony Janson, chief curator since September 1989, also resigns, as does Anne Jones, director of Development. Secretary McCain and

the trustees appoint Associate Director Heyward H. McKinney as acting director and John W. Coffey, currently the curator of American and modern art, as acting chief curator.

TO 2000: A PLAN TO ADVANCE THE NCMA, 1994 – 1996

"Being chosen to lead the North Carolina Museum of Art at this extraordinary moment in its history and in the history of the American art museum movement is a privilege and an opportunity of the highest order."

—*Lawrence J. Wheeler, Museum Director, 1994–present*

1994 Many visitors consider *A Gift to America: Masterpieces of European Paintings from the Samuel H. Kress Collection* the most outstanding show the Museum has sponsored since its opening in 1956. The North Carolina Museum of Art, the Museum of Fine Arts in Houston, the Seattle Art Museum, and the Fine Arts Museums of San Francisco co-sponsored the exhibition.[76]

Co-organized by David Steel, curator of European art, the exhibition opens in early February. The number of visitors, 59,000, is the second highest total for the Museum. (*Robes of Elegance*, shown in 1988, drew the greatest number of visitors — 70,000.) April is the second busiest month in the history of the Museum,

exceeded only by April 1983, the month the new building opened.

Much of the success of the Kress opening gala is due to the efforts of the Art Society members who organized and coordinated many of the programs and activities of the evening. At the gala, Department of Cultural Resources Secretary Betty Ray McCain announces the Humber Lecture Series, substantially funded by Egbert L. Davis, Jr.[77] The inaugural lecture in this series, in November 1994, is delivered by Jonathan Brown, professor at the Institute of Fine Arts at New York University.

With the support and efforts of its three boards, the Museum successfully completes Phase I of the Capital Cam-

paign. Under the leadership of Mazie and Jake Froelich, the Capital Campaign Steering Committee, along with loyal Museum patrons, raises more than $2 million. The funds will support future acquisition and education endowments and the Park Theater, the first phase of the *Art + Landscape* project. Representatives of the Art Society, the Museum Foundation, the Museum Board, and the New York design team participate in numerous local Capital Campaign fund-raising events in Hickory, Southern Pines, Winston-Salem, and several other cities in the state.[78]

Generous donors to the Park Theater are Veronese B. Atkins, David R. Hayworth, Joseph M. Bryan, Jr., Thomas S. Kenan III, and Burroughs Wellcome Company. Dona-

1.	Director Lawrence Wheeler with his first acquisition for the NCMA, Anselm Kiefer's *Untitled*.

2.	(left to right) Peggy Corbitt, Jake Froelich, Ivie Clayton, and Mazie Froelich of the Capital Campaign steering committee.

3.	At the opening of *A Gift to America: Masterpieces of European Painting from the Samuel H. Kress Collection*, Secretary Betty Ray McCain (at podium) introduces Mrs. Rush H. Kress (behind podium). Mrs. Kress also attended the original opening of the Kress donation to the NCMA at the Morgan Street location in 1960.

4.	Museum employees pack Batoni's *The Triumph of Venice*, one of the Kress gifts to the NCMA permanent collection, for shipment to another venue on the tour.

tions to the Veronese B. Atkins-endowed curatorial chair and a substantial gift from the Dickson Foundation for an art-acquisition endowment support the Museum's education and acquisition programs. Donations from the Brown F. Finch Foundation to the Art Trust Fund, created in 1970, also support these programs.

In October, Lawrence J. Wheeler becomes director of the North Carolina Museum of Art. He was previously deputy secretary of the North Carolina Department of Cultural Resources from 1977 until 1985, when he became assistant museum director and development director at the Cleveland Museum of Art. In assuming his new position, Wheeler said: "Being chosen to lead the North Carolina Museum of Art at this extraordinary moment in its history and in the history of the American art museum movement is a privilege and an opportunity of the highest order."[79]

One of the first decisions made by the new director is to purchase, in December, an untitled triptych by the contemporary German artist Anselm Kiefer, described by Acting Chief Curator John Coffey as "one of the most powerful and ambitious artists of our time."[80] The decision to purchase this painting underscores the Museum's intent to build a modern collection that is both national and international in scope and quality.

In late 1994, the Museum presents an exhibition of urban paintings, *New York, New York: Recent Cityscapes*. The show features new work from four New York artists: Martha Diamond, Jane Dickson, Yvonne Jacquette, and David Kapp. Huston Paschal organizes the exhibition and writes several essays for the catalogue, which includes contributions from photographer and writer John Rosenthal.

Activities at the Museum set new records in 1994. Docents contribute a record number of hours to the Museum; outreach volunteers number 198 in 65 counties; and tours for school children show an increase. Participation by African-Americans in Museum programs and activities increases, following considerable assistance from the Museum's African-American Advisory Board (orga-

"The arrival of Lawrence Wheeler on the scene in 1994 was a special boost to the membership growth aspirations of the Art Society."
— Rollie Tillman

"The Museum is the crown jewel of North Carolina culture, with a wonderful collection and fine volunteers committing their time, talents, and resources to the Museum. It's just a very exciting and satisfying place to be a part of."
— Ann Turner

nized in 1992) and volunteers. The Kwanzaa festival, which takes place at the Museum each December, is one of the largest Kwanzaa celebrations in the Triangle area.

Membership dues contribute almost one-third of the private funds that support the Museum's operating budget. The Contemporaries membership group promises a five-year pledge of $50,000 toward the Museum Park Theater project.

Two newly published brochures describing NCMA educational services for schools and the outside conservation services program become available at no cost. The number of conservation services clients increases, and in 1994 includes the Ackland Art Museum, Duke University

Museum of Art, Hickory Museum of Art, National Society of Colonial Dames of North Carolina in New Hanover County, and North Carolina Central University.

The NCMA receives two major grants during the year. The Institute of Museum Services awards $112,500 for general operating support, funds which the Museum plans to use to expand education and outreach programs in the state, as well as programs in the Museum Park Theater.

The Museum also receives a grant from the Samuel H. Kress Foundation in its continuing support of art conservation.

1995 In April—forty-eight years after the General Assembly approved a $1 million appropriation to purchase an art collection for North Carolina—the NCMA breaks ground for the Museum Park Theater. This innovative plan is itself an aesthetic statement, with its primary artistic element created by artist Barbara Kruger. The artist chose the phrase PICTURE THIS to become part of the landscape, through letters created from a wide variety of sculptural materials, such as blue stone, yellow pine, and indigenous plantings. The Park Theater will host a variety of musical and dramatic performances, lectures, educational workshops, and outdoor films. It will also serve as a picnic area and a site where visitors can discover

1.　　　The Kwanzaa festival, which occurs every December at the Museum, always features exciting dance performances.

2.　　　The size and multiple media of Anselm Kiefer's triptych *Untitled* made it a challenge for the installation team.

3.　　　State and Museum officials, donors, and the director take part in the ground-breaking for the Museum Park Theater. (left to right) Veronese Atkins, Betsy Buford, Lawrence Wheeler, Dennis Wicker, Betty Ray McCain, Gov. and Mrs. Jim Hunt, Terry Sanford, and Mazie and Jake Froelich enjoy the event.

4.　　　The unique design of the Joseph M. Bryan, Jr. Theater in the Museum Park gradually becomes a reality.

4.

art within the landscape. The anticipated completion date of the Park Theater facility is summer 1996.

In recognition of the NCMA's growth, the 1995 General Assembly approves an appropriation of $250,000 for the planning of additional space for programs and the collection.

Director Lawrence J. Wheeler, together with the staff and board of trustees, establishes long-range goals for the Museum. The strategy, "To 2000: A Plan to Advance the North Carolina Museum of Art," establishes four areas of focus: "(1) the need to embrace new technologies as we extend and expand knowledge about our collections; (2) the need to broaden the base of public participation and sup-

port; (3) the need to create collaborations with other educational and visual arts organizations; and (4) the need to develop additional space for education, public programs, and exhibitions."[81]

Twelve years after its 1983 opening, changes in the building become necessary. The areas selected for improvement are the staff entrance and reception area, and the art reference library. Money for these projects comes from the settlement of a ten-year lawsuit between the state and Middlesex Construction Company, the contractor for the new building. In settlement the state had received $525,000 and, after retaining $75,000 to pay for legal fees incurred, deposited $450,000 in a capital improvement fund

for use by the Museum. As part of its fiftieth anniversary celebration in 1996 – 97, the Museum plans to redesign and renovate the public information and shop areas with a portion of this money.

Gordon Hanes, a loyal friend and leading patron of the Museum, dies in August 1995. Hanes was a member of the board of trustees for eighteen years and board chairman from 1980 to 1987. Terry Sanford, board chairman, states that, "no person in the development of the Museum . . . had contributed more or had a greater love for the Museum than Gordon Hanes."[82]

A resolution adopted by the board of trustees in appreciation and memory of Hanes reads in part: "Gordon truly took

the Museum's mission to heart. He encouraged an interest in and an appreciation for art among many people through his unparalleled contributions to the Museum and its collections. Gifts of more than 130 works from Gordon and Copey Hanes have enhanced virtually every area of the Museum's collection . . . ."[83]

The trustees establish a new title, Trustee Emeritus, and name the following trustees as charter members: Veronese Atkins, Gordon Hanes (named posthumously), Abram Kanof, Mrs. Dan K. Moore, Beth Cummings Paschal, Mary Semans, and Egbert L. Davis, Jr.

Additions made to the collection in 1995 focus on ancient and contemporary art. With funds provided by the Art Soci-

ety through the Phifer Bequest, the Museum acquires the Roman bronze sculpture *Head of a Woman in the Guise of a Goddess.* This work fills a void in the classical collection. Another acquisition is *New Orleans: Ragging Home,* by North Carolina-born artist Romare Bearden.

The Museum also receives two contemporary paintings as gifts from the American Academy of Arts and Letters. Cheryl Goldsleger's *Colonnade* and David Kapp's *Ascending* add yet another dimension to the contemporary collection.

In 1995, exhibitions begin with *Dutch and Flemish Drawings from the Royal Library, Windsor Castle.* (The Museum and the Royal Library, represented by Mary-Theresa Morton, collaborated in organiz-

ing the exhibition, which opened at the Montreal Museum of Fine Arts and traveled to the Indianapolis Museum of Art following its presentation in Raleigh.) It is the first full-scale exhibition of the Queen's private collection of drawings by artists of the Low Countries, and includes works by Rubens and van Dyck. Christopher White, director of the Ashmolean Museum, Oxford University, is author of the catalogue. David Steel, the NCMA's curator of European art, coordinates the exhibition in Raleigh.

During the summer, *Passionate Visions of the American South: Self-Taught Artists from 1940 to the Present* is on view. Organized by the New Orleans Museum of Art, the exhibition at the Museum

4.

6.

"I use common objects and give a symbolic meaning. I always tell a story and I always try to give it balance. Life is made up of nights and days, sweet and sour things. The balance—I'm always seeking the balance."
—John Biggers

4.　　　John Biggers and his wife before one of the artist's monumental paintings.

5.　　　Murals inspired by the Biggers exhibition were created by North Carolina students and displayed in the Museum.

6.　　　Bob Chamblee (with clubs) won the Northwestern Mutual *Million Dollar Shoot-out*, a fund-raiser for the Museum.

includes additional loans of works by North Carolina artists and is coordinated by David Steel.

A retrospective exhibition celebrating the fifty-year career of North Carolina native John Biggers opens at the end of 1995. Painter, muralist, and sculptor, Biggers taught at Texas State University in Houston for thirty years. During the three months this exhibition is on view, the Museum conducts its largest outreach effort to date. Outreach activities include mural workshops, gallery and classroom study programs, receptions, and lectures. The Z. Smith Reynolds Foundation provides $25,000 for outreach programs associated with this exhibition, organized by the Museum of Fine Arts in Houston.

NCMA Associate Curator Huston Paschal coordinates the exhibition in Raleigh.

A significant fund-raiser for the year, supported by the Business Friends Council, is the Northwestern Mutual Million Dollar Shoot-out—the Museum's first corporate fund-raising event and one of the most successful fund-raisers in its history. The event nets more than $25,000, with more than 2,000 participants during the four-day golf competition. An equally successful fund-raiser this year is the Art Society's biennial Bal de Mer.

To consolidate its fund-raising, marketing, and public relations activities, the Museum creates a new position of director of external affairs. Georganne C. Bingham assumes the position in autumn

1995. Before joining the staff she worked most recently as a senior consultant for Systems Support Services in Charlotte.

The Museum wins design awards for several publications, including the *Calendar of Events*, the catalogue and invitation for the Kress Collection exhibition, and the catalogue for the *New York, New York* exhibition.

1996 In February, the Museum receives its five millionth visitor since opening in 1956.

The North Carolina Art Society celebrates its seventieth anniversary in 1996. Every NCMA member automatically holds membership in the North Carolina Art Society.

In June, the Museum opens the forty-seventh *North Carolina Artists Exhibition*. Guest curator Linda Shearer, director of the Williams College Museum of Art in Williamstown, Massachusetts, reviewed 2,254 slides submitted by 590 artists residing in North Carolina before selecting 100 works created by 23 artists. Coordinating the exhibition's installation and catalogue are Huston Paschal, associate curator of modern art, and Michelle Mead Dekker, curatorial assistant.

Joseph M. Bryan, Jr., contributes a gift of $600,000 toward the completion of the Museum Park Theater. The Museum names the theater in honor of Bryan for supporting this phase of its growth.

During the summer, a new driveway leading from Blue Ridge Road to the Museum is completed, and a traffic light is installed at the turn-in. Veronese Atkins donates funds for landscaping adjacent to the new entrance and J. C. Raulston, director of the North Carolina State University Arboretum, provides additional trees for the project and recommends a landscape architect to work with the staff.[84]

The NCMA receives several other contributions from corporations, businesses, and individuals. Northern Telecom (now Nortel), already a loyal Museum supporter, donates a new state-of-the-art telecommunications system, which includes voice-mail, conferencing, speed-dialing, and other features. Nortel donates both the equipment and the installation, making this one of the largest non-art gifts-in-kind the NCMA has ever received.

The Crabtree Valley merchant's association contributes items for a silent auction in Raleigh, donating more than $18,000 to the Museum.

Carolina Power & Light Company funds a learning center, which will help

> *"The Museum has been an important part of my life in Raleigh. The Art Society has not only been a pleasure to work with, but has played a major role in acclimating me to the pleasant sources of Southern culture."*
> — *Dr. Abram Kanof*

The *North Carolina Artists Exhibition 1996* displayed diverse concepts such as this installation by artist Austin Lowrey.

New tree plantings improve the Museum's entrance.

A couple enjoys a summer performance by the N.C. Symphony in the Joseph M. Bryan, Jr. Theater in the Museum Park.

3.

visitors learn about the permanent collection through self-directed computer programs. Designed for children and adults, the programs will be available for classroom or Internet use.

During the summer, the first events are presented in the Joseph M. Bryan, Jr. Theater. Performances by the Merce Cunningham Dance Company, Chuck Davis' African-American Dance Ensemble, and the North Carolina Symphony Orchestra inaugurate the theater in June and July.[85]

The NCMA Foundation Board of Directors, under the leadership of President Ivie L. Clayton, elects eight new members and creates several new committees. The committees and their chairpersons include: earned income, Jeanne Rauch; finance and development, Joseph M. Bryan, Jr.; and investment, Bruce Babcock. The foundation creates a fiftieth anniversary resources sub-committee with Suzanne McKinney named chairperson and a capital campaign planning committee, Ann Turner chairperson.

Abram Kanof, a Trustee Emeritus and adjunct curator of the Judaic collection, donates $50,000 to the Museum's research library in honor of his late wife, Dr. Frances Pascher Kanof.

Educational programs and outreach activities continue to reach many areas of the state. One of the most ambitious outreach programs is the mural workshop project related to the exhibition *The Art of John Biggers: View from the Upper Room*.

Approximately eight hundred students with their teachers from elementary, middle, and high schools participate in creating sixteen six-by-nine-foot murals. The Z. Smith Reynolds Foundation and the Kathleen Price Bryan Foundation support the exhibition and outreach projects.

A generous fiftieth anniversary gift from Wachovia Bank of North Carolina enables the staff of the Education Department to send art portfolios containing reproductions of twelve works in the Museum's collection to twenty-five hundred public schools in the state.

The Museum opens a Web site on the Internet. The site, called Art Net, provides users with online data about Museum events, exhibitions, and works of art in

1.

the permanent collection. The School of Design at North Carolina State University designs the site, while the Museum provides the content.

The Docent Endowment Lecture series presents artist Barbara Kruger as its annual speaker in 1996.[86]

Volunteers sponsor a perennial garden at the main entrance to the building. The volunteers also donate money for the purchase of selected equipment.

In late 1996, Dr. Abram Kanof, adjunct curator of Judaic art, supervises the redesign and reinstallation of the Judaic Gallery. He is assisted by John Coffey, chair of the Curatorial Department since 1995, and members of the Design Department. Dr. Kanof is also the author of *A Guide to*

the Judaic Art Collection.

In October, the NCMA presents a major retrospective of the work of Louis Rémy Mignot (1831–1870). Mignot was the only Southerner among the nineteenth-century Hudson River school of landscape painters. The exhibition officially opens the Museum's fiftieth anniversary celebration. It includes forty-eight paintings, from public and private collections nationwide, and is the first presentation of Mignot's work since a memorial show in 1876.

The exhibition and the accompanying monograph on the artist, published by the Smithsonian Institution Press for the NCMA, ends a three-year research project, supported by grants from the Henry Luce

Foundation and the NEA.[87] John Coffey and Katherine E. Manthorne, associat professor of art at the University of Illinois, Urbana-Champaign, are co-curator of the exhibition. After the exhibitio closes in Raleigh, it travels to the Nationa Academy of Design in New York.

As part of the Israel|North Carolin Cultural Exchange [88], the Museum pre sents the exhibition *Sepphoris in Galilee Crosscurrents of Culture* in Novembe Twenty-one of North Carolina's leadin arts institutions participate in the cultur exchange. The NCMA exhibition explore the art and architecture, religious tradi tions, and colorful history of Sepphoris, once vibrant city in Roman Palestine. catalogue of the exhibition and educa

2.

ional programs, at the NCMA and across the state, supplement the show. Co-cura- ors of the exhibition are Rebecca Martin Nagy and Professor Eric M. Meyers of the Department of Religion at Duke Universi- ty. Support for the project comes from the North Carolina Department of Cultural Resources, the State of Israel, Ministry of Foreign Affairs, and numerous other con- tributors.

With funds provided by the North Carolina Art Society (Phifer Bequest), the North Carolina Museum of Art Guild, and the sale of deaccessioned works of art, the Museum purchases a major abstract com- position, *Station (577-2),* by twentieth- century German painter Gerhard Richter.

Gifts during the year include a collec- tion of more than 125 pre-Columbian objects, from Dr. Clifton Mountain and Marilyn T. Mountain; and a group of ten American paintings, dating from 1944 to 1984. The paintings, a promised gift from Dr. and Mrs. Alan Leslie, include works by Hans Burkhardt, Stanton Macdonald- Wright, and Lee Mullican.

As 1996 ends, plans to celebrate the fiftieth anniversary are underway. Exhibi- tions, special events, lectures, educational and outreach programs, publications, con- certs, and performances will be presented as the new year unfolds. Publications include a special issue of the *Bulletin* devoted to German Expressionism to hon- or William R. Valentiner.

In association with John F. Blair, Pub- lisher, the NCMA is producing *The Store of Joys: Writers Celebrate the North Carolina Museum of Art's Fiftieth Anniversary.* The book contains contributions from forty- five of the state's writers, each of whom chose an object in the permanent collec- tion and wrote a response to it. Novelist and poet Reynolds Price chairs the pro- ject's advisory committee that includes writers Betty Adcock, Gerald Barrax, Doris Betts, Fred Chappell, and Allan Gurganus.

MANY REASONS TO CELEBRATE

"The people of North Carolina deserve a museum that is, in all its expressions, equal to its great collections."
—*Lawrence J. Wheeler*

The year-long celebratory observance of the fiftieth anniversary will pay homage to the 1947 North Carolina General Assembly and its wisdom in appropriating $1 million for the purchase of old master paintings. That action heralded the founding of the North Carolina Museum of Art, and the state became the first in the nation to set aside public funds to create an art collection for its people.

This occasion also honors the Kress Foundation for matching the $1 million state appropriation with the donation of more than seventy paintings and sculptures — the largest Kress gift to any regional museum.

The celebration will pay tribute as well to every individual, business, group, and foundation that has contributed to the success of the North Carolina Museum of Art.

The collection today, considered one of the best in the southeastern United States, numbers some 5,600 works of art. Included are paintings, sculpture, and other works representing the achievements of 5,000 years of human endeavor, from ancient Egypt to contemporary times. Since opening in 1956, more than 1,600 works of art from its collection have been lent to museums nationally and internationally — an average of 40 works per year. During the same period, approximately 19,000 works presented in nearly 350 exhibitions were borrowed from other institutions — an average of almost 9 exhibitions for each year.

Attendance in fiscal year 1995–96 reached 230,000.

The staff in 1996 numbers 102 full-time employees (88 funded by the state and 14 by the NCMA Foundation) and 14 part-time (8 funded by the state, 6 by the foundation). Nearly one-third of the employees work in Security.

Supplementing the Museum staff are 200 docent volunteers and 300 other volunteers.

The Museum currently has 224 outreach volunteers in 70 counties. They present slide programs, based on the permanent collection and special exhibitions, to schools, cultural and civic clubs, retirement homes, libraries, colleges

1.

"From the distance of retirement, I salute my colleagues who have been instrumental in bringing about the remarkable success story, which this document celebrates."
— *Gay Mahaffy Hertzman*

110–111

churches, and other groups across the state.

The operating budget for the fiscal year 1996 – 97 (not including expenditures for acquisitions) is approximately $6.7 million. The ratio of state-to-private funding varies annually. In fiscal year 1996 – 97 the ratio is approximately one-half state and one-half private funds administered by the NCMA Foundation.

The state Department of Administration assigns eight employees to the Museum to work in building systems engineering and grounds maintenance areas. In addition, the department pays the Museum's utility bills, estimated at $600,000 to $800,000 per year.

The Museum is an agency of the North Carolina Department of Cultural Resources, governed by a board of trustees consisting of twenty-eight members. Board members include those appointed by the governor, North Carolina General Assembly, North Carolina Art Society, NCMA Foundation, and NCMA Board of Trustees. The Art Society consists of a forty-member board of directors that represents Museum members in the governance of the institution, serves as a statewide advocacy group, and oversees the Robert F. Phifer Fund. The NCMA Foundation has thirty-one members on its board of directors and serves as the primary steward of all private funds received by the Museum. The foundation also supports educational programs, exhibitions, publications, the Museum shop and café, and fundraising efforts.

Working with space planning consultant M. Goodwin Associates, Inc., the Museum is developing a plan that will expand the building by 60,000 square feet and renovate the existing facility. Accordingly, it has engaged a fund-raising consultant, Ross, Johnston, and Kersting, Inc., to study the feasibility of a capital campaign to raise up to $20 million in donations.

APPENDIX

General Assembly, Act of 1929
1929 CHAPTER 314

An act placing the North Carolina State Art Society, Incorporated, under the patronage and control of the State of North Carolina.

CHAPTER 314
AN ACT TO PLACE THE NORTH CAROLINA STATE ART SOCIETY, INCORPORATED, UNDER THE PATRONAGE AND CONTROL OF THE STATE, TO MAKE PROVISION FOR THE EXHIBIT OF WORKS OF ART OWNED OR CONTROLLED BY IT, AND FOR OTHER PURPOSES.

Whereas, the North Carolina State Art Society, Incorporated, is an organization of citizens of this State interested in promoting an appreciation of art among our people and particularly in the establishment of a State art museum, with suitable buildings and exhibits; and

Whereas, said Society has already received a number of valuable gifts and will probably receive many others; and

Whereas, it is desired by said Society and its members to place it under the patronage and control of the State to the end that persons who contemplate making gifts to it and for the establishment of a State art museum may be assured of the interest and concern of the State Government in these objects, and of the willingness of the State to cooperate in safe-guarding the works of art now owned or to be acquired by it, and in promoting their enjoyment by all classes of our people; now, therefore.

THE GENERAL ASSEMBLY OF NORTH CAROLINA DO ENACT:

SECTION 1. That the governing body of the North Carolina State Art Society, Incorporated, shall be a board of directors consisting of sixteen members, of whom the Governor of the State, the Superintendent of Public Instruction, the Attorney General, and the chairman of the art committee of the North Carolina Federation of Women's Clubs shall be ex-officio members, and four others shall be named by the Governor of the state. The remaining eight directors shall be chosen by the members of the North Carolina State Art Society, Incorporated, in such manner and for such terms as that body shall determine.

SEC. 2. Of the four directors first named by the Governor, two shall be appointed for terms of two years each and two for terms of four years each, and subsequent appointments shall be made for terms of four years each.

SEC. 3. That the said board of directors, when organized under the terms of this act, shall have authority to adopt the by-laws for the society, and said by-laws shall thereafter be subject to change only by a three-fifths vote of a quorum of said board of directors at two consecutive regular meeting.

SEC. 4. The Board of Public Buildings and Grounds is authorized and empowered to set apart, for the exhibition of works of art owned, donated or loaned to the North Carolina State Art Society, Incorporated, any space in any of the public buildings in the city of Raleigh which may be so used without interference with the conduct of the business of the State, and it shall be the duty of the custodians of such buildings to care for, safeguard and protect such exhibits and works of art.

SEC. 5. It shall be the duty of the State Auditor to make an annual audit of the accounts of the North Carolina State Art Society, Incorporated, and to make report thereof to the General Assembly at each of its regular sessions.

SEC. 6. This act shall be in force and effect from and after its ratification.

Ratified this the 19th day of March, A. D. 1929.

General Assembly, Act of 1947
1947 CHAPTER 1097

An act relating to the State Art Society and making appropriations thereto
for special purposes.

CHAPTER 1097
S. B. 395
AN ACT RELATING TO THE STATE ART SOCIETY AND TO MAKE APPROPRIATIONS THERETO
FOR SPECIAL PURPOSES.

THE GENERAL ASSEMBLY OF NORTH CAROLINA DO ENACT:

SECTION 1. Chapter 140 of the General Statutes of North Carolina is hereby amended by
adding a new Article, to Article 1, and to be designated as Article 1A, as follows:

ART. 1a. Acquisition and Preservation of Works of Art.

SEC. 140-5.1. Purpose of Article. The North Carolina State Art Society is authorized and empowered to
inspect, appraise, obtain attributions and evaluations, to purchase, acquire, transport, exhibit, loan and
store, and to receive on consignment or as loans, statuary, paintings and other works of art of any and
every kind and description which are worthy of acquisition and preservation, and to do all other things
incidental to and necessary to effectuate the purposes of this Article.

SEC. 140-5.2. Preservation of Works of Art. The North Carolina State Art Society shall be responsible
for the care, custody, storage and preservation of all works of art acquired by it, or received by
consignment or loan.

SEC. 140-5.3. Right to Receive Gifts. In order to carry out the purposes of this Article, the North
Carolina State Art Society is authorized to acquire by gift or will, absolutely or in trust, from individuals,
corporations, the Federal Government or from any other source, works of art or money or other
property, which might be retained, sold or otherwise used to promote the purposes of the North
Carolina State Art Society; provided that works of art acquired by the Society under the provision of this
Section may not be pledged, mortgaged or sold; and provided, further, that any gifts, donations, devises,
bequests, or legacies of property, other than works of art, money and bonds may be disposed of only with
the approval of the Governor and Council of State. The proceeds of the sale of any property acquired
under the provisions of this Section shall be deposited in the State Treasury to the account of the State
Art Society Special Fund.

SEC. 140-5.4. Special Fund. Gifts of money to the North Carolina State Art Society, when made for the
purposes of this Article, shall be paid in to the State Treasury and maintained as a fund to be designated;
State Art Society Special Fund. All gifts made to the North Carolina State Art Society shall be exempt
from every form of taxation including, but not by way of limitation, ad valorem, intangible, gift,
inheritance and income taxation.

SEC. 140-5.5. Appropriation Contingent on Gifts. There is hereby appropriated out of any
unappropriated General Fund surplus that may exist at June 30, 1947, the sum of one million dollars
($1,000,000.00) which appropriation shall not be made available for expenditure until funds are
available to meet all appropriations made for the biennium 1947 – 49 and until the sum of one million
dollars ($1,000,000.000) shall have been secured through gifts and paid into the State Treasury to the
credit of the special fund "State Art Society Special Fund". The appropriations contained herein and the
receipts collected under the provisions of this Act shall be subject to the provisions of the Executive
Budget Act.

SEC. 140.5.6. Expenditure of Funds. After the conditions set forth in Section 140-5.5 shall have been complied with, the sum of one million dollars ($1,000,000.00) appropriated in Section 140-5.5 and the sum of one million dollars ($1,000,000.00) in gifts paid in to the State Treasury for the State Art Society for the purposes set out in Sections 140-5.1, and 140-5.2 and for all necessary expenses incidental thereto, including actual necessary expenses and subsistence as may be incurred in travel for the purpose of inspecting prospective gifts and purchases, such expenditures to be made only by a Commission of five members to be appointed by the Governor from the membership of the North Carolina State Art Society, which Commission shall be known as the "State Art Commission". The State Treasurer shall, with the approval of the Governor and Council of State, invest any unexpended moneys in the State Art Society Special Fund in securities authorized to be purchased for the Sinking Funds of the State of North Carolina.

Two of the members of said Commission shall be appointed for a term of one year, three members shall be appointed for a term of two years, and thereafter the term for all members of the Commission shall be two years. Any vacancy arising on the Commission shall be filled by appointment by the Governor for the unexpired portion of the term.

SEC. 140-5.7. Expenses of Commission. The members of the Commission described in Section 140-5.6 shall serve without compensation, but in attending meetings of the Commission the members shall be paid such actual necessary expenses as may be incurred in travel and subsistence while attending such meetings not in excess of that allowed by the biennial appropriation Act.

SEC. 1 1/2. In the event of the erection of a State Art Museum under the provisions of this Act, the same shall be erected in the City of Raleigh.

SEC. 2. All laws and clauses of laws in conflict with this Act are hereby repealed.

SEC. 3. This Act shall become effective upon its ratification.

In the General Assembly read three times and ratified, this the 5th day of April, 1947.

Works of Art Purchased with the $1 Million State of North Carolina Appropriation

52.9.1 Ralph Albert Blakelock
American, 1847 – 1919
Sunrise, 1868.

52.9.2 Charles F. Blauvelt
American, 1824 – 1900
A German Immigrant Inquiring His Way, 1855.

52.9.3 David G. Blythe
American, 1815 – 1865
A Match Seller, 1859.

52.9.4 George Loring Brown
American, 1814 – 1889
Morning, View on Smith's Island, Norwalk Bay, Connecticut, 1863.

52.9.5 John G. Brown
American, 1831 – 1913
A Tough Story, 1886.

52.9.6 John G. Brown
American, 1831 – 1913
The Blacksmith, c. 1900.

52.9.7 Thomas Cole
American, 1801 – 1848
Romantic Landscape, c. 1826.

52.9.8 John Singleton Copley
American (active in Great Britain from 1774), 1738 – 1815
Sir William Pepperrell (1746 – 1816) and His Family, 1778.

52.9.9 Jasper Francis Cropsey
American, 1823 – 1900
Eagle Cliff, Franconia Notch, New Hampshire, 1858.

52.9.10 Thomas Doughty
American, 1793 – 1856,
Early Winter, c. 1853.

52.9.11 Frank Duveneck
American, 1848 – 1919
Mrs. Mary E. Goddard ("The Crimson Gown"), 1879.

52.9.12 Ralph E. W. Earl
American, 1785/88 – 1838
Andrew Jackson, c. 1830 – 32.

52.9.13 John Adams Elder
American, 1833 – 1895
Jefferson Davis.

52.9.14 Samuel L. Gerry
American, 1813 – 1891
The Snow Line, Mount Washington, 1855.

52.9.15 Thomas Hicks
American, 1823 – 1890
The Musicale, Barber Shop, Trenton Falls, New York, 1866.

52.9.16 Winslow Homer
American, 1836 – 1910
Weaning the Calf, 1875.

52.9.17 George Inness
American, 1825 – 1894
Under the Greenwood, 1881.

52.9.18 John Wesley Jarvis
American, 1780 – 1840
John Quincy Adams.

52.9.19 Eastman Johnson
American, 1824 – 1906
The Blacksmith Shop.

52.9.20 William Keith
American, 1839 – 1911
Mono Pass, Sierra Nevada Mountains, California, 1877.

52.9.21 George Lambdin
American, 1830 – 1896
The Amateur Circus, 1869.

52.9.23 Christian Mayr
American, born Germany, 1805 – 1851
Kitchen Ball at White Sulphur Springs, Virginia, 1838.

52.9.24 William Morgan
American, 1826 – 1900
The Organ Grinder.

52.9.25 William Tylee Ranney
American, 1813 – 1857
First News of the Battle of Lexington, 1847.

52.9.27 Junius B. Stearns
American, 1810 – 1885
Watering Horses, 1852.

52.9.28 Maurice Sterne
American, born Latvia, 1878 – 1957
Dance of the Elements, Bali, 1913.

52.9.29 Unknown
British
King George III, c. 1775.

52.9.30 Unknown
British
Queen Charlotte, c. 1775.

52.9.31 Gilbert Stuart
American, 1755 – 1828
Mr. Charles Davis, 1808.

52.9.32 Gilbert Stuart
American, 1755 – 1828
Mrs. Charles Davis, née Eliza Bussey (1783 – 1841), 1808.

52.9.33 Unknown, School of Haarlem
Dutch, active first half of the 16th century
The Adoration of the Magi, c. 1525 – 1550.

52.9.36 After Aelbert Cuyp
Dutch, 1620 – 1691
Landscape with Figures and Cattle, c. 1660 – 1665.

52.9.37 Attributed to Jacob van Spreeuwen
Dutch, 1611 – after 1658
The Scholar and His Visitor, c. 1630 – 35.

52.9.38 Jacob Duck
Dutch, c. 1600 – 1667
Soldiers' Quarters, c. 1635.

52.9.39 Gerbrand van den Eeckhout
Dutch, 1621 – 1674
The Expulsion of Hagar and Ishmael, 1666.

52.9.41 Govert Flinck
Dutch, 1615 – 1660
The Return of the Prodigal Son, c. 1640.

52.9.42 Jan Hals
Dutch, active 1635 – 1674
Portrait of a Gentleman, 1644.

52.9.43 Jan Jansz. den Uyl
Dutch, 1605/6 – 1639/40
Vanitas Banquet Piece, c. 1635.

52.9.44 Melchior D'Hondecoeter
Dutch, 1636 – 1695
Barnyard Scene.

52.9.45 Pieter de Hooch
Dutch, 1629 – 1684
The Fireside, c. 1670 – 75.

52.9.46 Ludolf de Jongh
Dutch, 1616 – 1679
Soldiers at Reveille, 1655 – 58.

52.9.47 Nicolaes Maes
Dutch, 1634 – 1693
Captain Job Jansz. Cuyter and His Family, 1659.

52.9.48 Michiel van Mierevelt
Dutch, 1567 – 1641
Portrait of a Lady, 1633.

52.9.49 Michiel van Mierevelt
Dutch, 1567 – 1641
Portrait of a Man, 1633.

52.9.50 Jan Miense Molenaer
Dutch, 1610 – 1668
The Dentist, 1629.

52.9.51 Attributed to Aert van der Neer
Dutch, 1603 – 1677
Canal Scene in Moonlight, c. 1660 – 1665.

52.9.53 Isack van Ostade
Dutch, 1621 – 1649
Peasants Gathered Outside an Inn, 1642.

52.9.54 Willem de Poorter
Dutch, 1608 – 1648
A Man Weighing Gold, c. 1635.

52.9.55 Jan Lievens
Dutch, 1607 – 1674
The Feast of Esther, c. 1625 – 26.

52.9.56 Jacob van Ruisdael
Dutch, 1628/29 – 1682
Wooded Landscape with Waterfall, c. 1665 – 1670.

52.9.57 Willem van Aelst
Dutch, 1626 – after 1682
Vanitas Flower Piece, c. 1656.

52.9.58 Jan Steen
Dutch, 1625 – 1679
The Worship of the Golden Calf,
c. 1671 – 72.

52.9.59 Matthias Stomer
Dutch, c. 1600 – after 1643
The Adoration of the Shepherds,
c. 1635 – 40.

52.9.60 Adriaen van de Velde
Dutch, 1636 – 1672
Exercising a Horse, c. 1658.

52.9.61 Esaias van de Velde
Dutch, 1587 – 1630
Winter Scene, 1614.

52.9.63 Pieter Boel
Flemish, 1622 – 1674
Still Life with Swan, 1657.

52.9.64 Philips Wouwermans
Dutch, 1619 – 1668
The Deer Hunt, c. 1665.

52.9.65 William Beechey
British, 1753 – 1839
The Oddie Children, 1789.

52.9.66 William Beechey
British, 1753 – 1839
Thomas Lowndes, 1823.

52.9.67 Francis Cotes
British, 1726 – 1770
James Duff, 2nd Earl of Fife, 1765.

52.9.68 Thomas Gainsborough
British, 1727 – 1788
*Master Drummond on
Horseback*.

52.9.69 Thomas Gainsborough
British, 1727 – 1788
The Earl of Buckinghamshire.

52.9.72 John de Critz
British, 1555 – 1641
Lady Arabella Stuart, c. 1590.

52.9.74 John Hoppner
British, 1758 – 1810
*William Wyndham, Lord
Grenville*.

52.9.76 Thomas Hudson
British, 1701 – 1779
Mrs. Cooper and Her Children.

52.9.77 Thomas Lawrence
British, 1769 – 1830
Mrs. John Halkett, c. 1802.

52.9.78 Martin Archer Shee
British, 1769 – 1850,
Portrait of a Gentleman, 1815-30.

52.9.82 Joshua Reynolds
British, 1723 – 1792
Miss Anna Maria Patten, 1764.

52.9.84 George Romney
British, 1734 – 1802
Lt. Colonel James Hartley,
1783 – 89.

52.9.85 George Romney
British, 1734 – 1802
Lady Ramsay, 1786 – 87.

52.9.86 George Romney
British, 1734 – 1802
*Elizabeth, Margravine of
Anspach*, 1797.

52.9.88 Pieter Brueghel, The Younger
Flemish, 1564/5 – 1637/38
Peasants at a Roadside Inn,
c. 1600 – 25.

52.9.89 Follower of Bernard van Orley
Flemish, 1492 – 1542
The Ascension, c. 1525 – 30.

52.9.90 Follower of Bernard van Orley
Flemish, 1492 – 1542
The Pentecost, c. 1525 – 30.

52.9.91 Ambrosius Benson
Flemish, 1510 – 1550
Man with a Quill, c. 1540's.

52.9.92 Jan Brueghel, the Elder
Flemish, 1568 – 1625
*Harbor Scene with St. Paul's
Departure from Caesarea*, 1596.

52.9.93 Unknown
Italian, Umbrian
Cassone, c. 1500.

52.9.95 Follower of Anthony van Dyck
Flemish, 1599 – 1641
Erycius Puteanus, c. 1629.

52.9.96 Follower of Anthony van Dyck
Flemish, 1599 – 1641
*Prince Charles Louis (1617 – 80)
and Prince Rupert (1619 – 82)*,
1636 – 37.

52.9.97 Follower of Anthony van Dyck
Flemish, 1599 – 1641
Triumph of the Infant Bacchus,
1622 – 27.

52.9.98 Unknown
Flemish
The Creation, c. 1600.

52.9.99 Jacob Jordaens
Flemish, 1593 – 1678
*Jupiter & Mercury in the House of
Philemon and Baucis*, c. 1645.

52.9.100 Jacob Jordaens
Flemish, 1593 – 1678
Christ and the Pharisees,
1660 – 70.

52.9.102 Circle of Hans Memling
Flemish, c. 1433 – 1494
Christ on the Cross, c. 1480.

52.9.103 Joos de Momper
Flemish, 1564 – 1635
Landscape with a Bridge, c. 1600.

52.9.104 Joos de Momper
Flemish, 1564 – 1635
Winter Landscape, c. 1620's.

52.9.106 Circle of Peter Paul Rubens
Flemish, 1577 – 1640
*Dr. Theodore Turquet de
Mayenne*, c. 1629 – 30.

52.9.107 Peter Paul Rubens and workshop
Flemish, 1577 – 1640
The Holy Family, 1633 – 35.

52.9.108 Peter Paul Rubens and Frans
Snyders Flemish, 1577 – 1640,
and 1579 – 1657
The Bear Hunt, 1639 – 40.

52.9.112 Gerard Seghers
Flemish, 1591 – 1651
The Denial of St. Peter, 1620 – 25.

52.9.113 Frans Snyders
Flemish, 1579 – 1657
Market Scene on a Quay, c. 1635.

52.9.114 Justus Sustermans
Flemish, 1597 – 1681
Portrait of a Child, c. 1670's.

52.9.115 David Teniers II (the Younger)
Flemish, 1610 – 1690
Dancers at a Village Inn, c. 1650.

52.9.116 David Teniers II (the Younger)
Flemish, 1610 – 1690
The Armorer's Shop, c. 1640 – 45.

52.9.117 David Teniers II (the Younger)
Flemish, 1610 – 1690
The Flight into Egypt, c.1660 – 65.

52.9.118 François Boucher
French, 1703 – 1770
Allegory of Music, 1752.

52.9.120 François Boucher
French, 1703 – 1770
*Landscape with a Castle and
a Mill*.

52.9.121 Flemish (?)
active 1st half of the 17th century
*Angel Freeing Saint Peter from
Prison*, 1625 – 30.

52.9.122 Studio of Jacques-Louis David
French, 1748 – 1825
Jacques-Louis David, 1790 – 1818.

52.9.123 François Desportes
French, 1661 – 1743
*Urn of Flowers with Fruits and
Hare*, 1715.

52.9.124 Anonymous Dutch Master
Dutch
Portrait of a Youth, 1634.

52.9.125 Claude Lorrain (Claude Gellée)
French, 1600 – 1682
*Landscape with Peasants
Returning with their Herds*,
c. 1637.

52.9.126 Jean Michelin
French, 17th century
*A Poultry Merchant and an Old
Woman*, 165(2?)

52.9.127 Pierre Mignard
French, 1612 – 1695, active in
Rome from 1635 – 1657
*Christ and the Woman of
Samaria*, 1681.

52.9.129 Follower of Jean-Marc Nattier
French, 1685 – 1766
Mademoiselle de Beaujolais,
18th century.

52.9.130 Follower of Jean-Marc Nattier
French, 1685 – 1766
*Portrait of a Lady as a Vestal
Virgin,* 1759.

52.9.133 Hans Brosamer
German, 1500 – 1554
*Portrait of Sebald Haller von
Hallerstein,* 1528.

52.9.134 Bartel Bruyn, the Younger
German, 1530 – 1610
Portrait of Heinrich Cruedener,
1580s.

52.9.135 Bartel Bruyn, the Younger
German, 1530 – 1610
*Portrait of the Wife of Heinrich,
Cruedener,* 1580 – 89.

52.9.136 Unknown
German
*Christ and the Woman of
Samaria,* c. 1450.

52.9.137 Unknown
German
Christ and the Adulteress, c. 1450.

52.9.138 Peter Gaertner
German, active c. 1524 – 1537
Hans Geyer, 1524.

52.9.140 Hans Mielich
German, 1516 – 1573
Portrait of a Man, 1543.

52.9.141 George Pencz
German, c.1500 – 1550
Portrait of Martin Luther, 1533.

52.9.142 Unknown
German
*St. Barbara and St. Valentine with
Caspar von Laubenberg and His
Sons,* c. 1450.

52.9.143 Unknown
German
*St. Catherine and St. Vitus with
Anna von Freiberg and Her
Daughters,* c. 1450.

52.9.145 Bernardo Bellotto
Italian, 1720 – 1780
*View of Dresden with the
Frauenkirche at Left,* 1747.

52.9.146 Bernardo Bellotto
Italian, 1720 – 1780
*View of Dresden with the
Hofkirche at Right,* 1748.

52.9.147 Faustino Bocchi
Italian, 1659 – 1742
*A Trial at Law among Animals
and Pygmies.*

52.9.148 Paris Bordon
Italian, 1500 – 1570
Portrait of a Man in Armor,
1535 – 40.

52.9.149 Antonio Canaletto
Italian, 1697 – 1768
*Capriccio: The Rialto Bridge and
the Church of S. Giorgio
Maggiore,* c. 1750.

52.9.150 Agostino Carracci
Italian, 1557 – 1602
Death of Actaeon, c. 1585.

52.9.151 Giovanni Benedetto Castiglione
Italian, 1609 – 1665
*Noah and the Animals Entering
the Ark,* 1630 – 32.

52.9.152 Giovanni Battista Cima
da Conegliano
Italian, 1459 – 1518
*Madonna and Child in a
Landscape,* 1496 – 99.

52.9.153 Giuseppe Maria Crespi
Italian, 1665 – 1747
The Resurrection of Christ,
c. 1690.

52.9.154 Pseudo Pier Francesco Fiorentino
Italian, active 1450 – 1500
Madonna and Child, c. 1480.

52.9.155 Workshop of Francesco Francia
Italian, 1450 – 1517
Madonna and Child,
c. 1495 – 1500.

52.9.156 Attributed to Giovanni Odazzi
Italian, 1663 – 1731
*Benedict XIII Consecrating S.
Giovanni in Laterano,* c. 1726.

52.9.157 Pier Leone Ghezzi
Italian, 1674 – 1755
The Lateran Convention of 1725,
1725.

52.9.158 Luca Giordano
Italian, 1632 – 1705
The Finding of Moses,
c. 1685 – 90.

52.9.160 Circle of Moretto da Brescia
Italian, 1498 – 1554
*Portrait of a Gentleman in Armor
on Horseback.*

52.9.161 Piedmont School
Italian
Adoration of the Shepherds,
1430 – 40.

52.9.162 Piedmont School
Italian
The Procession of the Magi,
1430 – 40.

52.9.163 Unknown
Italian, Ligurian, 16th century
Table.

52.9.164 Sebastiano Ricci
Italian, 1659 – 1734
The Continence of Scipio,
1708 – 10.

52.9.165 Sebastiano Ricci
Italian, 1659 – 1734
*Alexander and the Family of
Darius,* 1708 – 10.

52.9.166 After Sebastiano Ricci
Italian, 1659 – 1734
Flight into Egypt.

52.9.167 Andrea del Sarto and assistants
Italian, 1486 – 1530
*Madonna and Child with St. John
the Baptist,* c. 1525 – 28.

52.9.168 Bernardo Strozzi
Italian, 1581 – 1644
*St. Lawrence Distributing the
Treasures of the Church,* c. 1625.

52.9.169 Circle of Bartolomé Bermejo
Spanish, c. 1435/40 – 1500
*Portable Altarpiece: Pieta, Saints
Francis, Sebastian, John the
Evangelist, Jerome and John the
Baptist.*

52.9.170 Luis Borrassa
Spanish, 1360 – 1424
Christ before Pilate, c. 1420.

52.9.172 B. del Castro
Spanish, active c. 1500 – 1550
*Zemeyas, One of the Judges of
Christ,* c. 1510 – 20.

52.9.173 B. del Castro
Spanish, active c. 1500 – 1550
Joeth, One of the Judges of Christ,
c. 1510 – 20.

52.9.178 Bartolomé Murillo
Spanish, 1617/18 – 1682
*The Blessed Giles before Pope
Gregory IX,* 1645 – 46.

52.9.179 Anonymous
Spanish
Esau Selling His Birthright,
after 1830.

52.9.180 Esteban Márquez de Velasco
Spanish, died 1696
The Marriage of the Virgin,
c. 1690 – 95.

52.9.181 Pedro Orrente
Spanish, 1580 – 1643
*Jacob Conjuring Laban's
Sheep,* 1612 – 22.

52.9.183 Jusepe de Ribera
Spanish, 1591 – 1652
St. John the Baptist, c. 1624.

52.9.190 School of Francisco de
Zurbarán
Spanish, 1598 – 1664
Flowers, Fruit, Vegetables,
c. 1650.

52.9.192/A-B Unknown
Italian
Pair of Candlesticks, c. 1600.

52.9.193 Unknown
Indian
Madras Chair, c. 1770.

52.9.195/1-2 Unknown
Flemish
Easter Candlesticks,
16th century.

52.9.196 Adolf Ulric Wertmüller
American, 1751 – 1811
Portrait of a Man (Samuel Donaldson ?), c. 1795.

52.9.201 Frans Snyders
Flemish, 1579 – 1657
Still Life with a Grey Parrot, c. 1625 – 35.

52.9.202 Elliott Daingerfield
American, 1859 – 1932
The Grand Canyon, c. 1912.

52.9.203 Workshop of Antonio Vivarini
Italian, 1416 – 1484
St. Louis of Toulouse.

52.9.204 Workshop of Antonio Vivarini
Italian, 1416 – 1484
St. John the Baptist.

52.9.205 Circle of Jacob Esselens
Dutch, 1626 – 1687
Calm Sea, c. 1650's.

52.9.207 Follower of Peter Paul Rubens
Flemish, 1577 – 1640
Gideon Overcoming the Midianites, c. 1616.

52.9.208 Unknown
Italian
Florentine Chair, one of a pair, 15th century.

52.9.209 Unknown
Italian
Florentine Chair, one of a pair, 15th century.

52.9.210 Unknown
Italian
Florentine Chair, one of a pair, 16th century.

52.9.211 Unknown
Italian
Florentine Chair, one of a pair, 16th century.

52.9.212 Unknown
Italian
Low Chair,(sgabello), 16th century.

52.9.213 François de Nomé, called Monsu Desiderio
French, c. 1593 – after 1644
The Martyrdom of Saint Januarius, (Gennaro), 1622.

52.9.214 Unknown
Italian
Low Chair, (Sgabello), 16th century.

52.9.215 Unknown
Flemish
Gothic Chest, 15th century.

52.9.216 Unknown
French
Chair, 16th century.

52.9.218 Unknown
French
Chair, one of a pair, style of Henry II, 1519–59.

52.9.219 Unknown
French
Chair, one of a pair, style of Henry II, 1519 – 59.

52.9.220 Unknown
French
Chair, one of a pair, 17th century.

52.9.221 Unknown
French
Chair, one of a pair, 17th century.

52.9.222 Unknown
Italian
Cassone, 16th century.

52.9.223 Unknown
Italian
Cassone, 16th century.

52.9.224 Elisabeth Louise Vigée Lebrun
French, 1755 – 1842
Count Ivan Ivanovitch Chouvaloff, c. 1795 – 97.

52.9.225 Sienese School
Italian
Madonna and Child, c. 1445 – 55.

52.9.226 Unknown
French
Female Flutist, 18th century.

52.9.228 Unknown
German
Gothic Chest, 15th century.

52.9.229 Maurice Sterne
American, born Latvia, 1878 – 1957
Higgins Pier, c. 1945.

52.9.231 -232 Unknown
Spanish
A pair of iron gates.

Works of Art Purchased by the Art Commission in 1953 with Funds from the North Carolina Art Society (Robert F. Phifer Bequest)

52.9.26 Albert Pinkham Ryder
American, 1847 – 1917
The Pasture, 1875 – 80.

52.9.34 Thomas Moran
American, 1837 – 1926
Fiercely the red sun descending/Burned his way across the heavens, c. 1875.

52.9.73 Circle of Marc Gheeraerts
British, 1561 – 1635
Portrait of a Man, c. 1603.

52.9.79 Thomas Lawrence and studio
British, 1769 – 1830
Lady Louisa Harvey (1758 – 1841) and Her Children, Edward and Louisa, begun 1793.

52.9.94 Follower of Anthony van Dyck
Flemish, 1599 – 1641
Henry Prince of Wales.

52.9.105 Master of the Female Half-Lengths
Flemish, active c. 1525 – 1550
The Flight into Egypt, c. 1530 – 35.

52.9.128 Jean François Millet
French, 1814 – 1875
Peasant Spreading Manure, 1854 – 55.

52.9.131 Jean-Baptiste Oudry
French, 1686 – 1755
Swan Attacked by a Dog, 1745.

52.9.132 Studio of Hyacinthe Rigaud
French, 1659 – 1743
Louis XV (1710 – 1774), c. 1715 – 17.

52.9.139 Attributed to Stefan Lochner
German, c.1405 – 1451
St. Jerome in His Study, c. 1440.

52.9.171 Circle of Francisco de Zurbarán
Spanish, 1598 – 1664
Still Life with Glass, Fruit,and Jar, c. 1650.

52.9.174 After Luis Egidio Meléndez
Spanish, 1716 – 1780
Still Life with Fruit, Cheese, and a Pitcher,after c. 1830.

52.9.175 After Luis Egidio Meléndez
Spanish, 1716 – 1780
Still Life with Bread, Jug, and a Napkin, after c. 1830.

52.9.176 Luis Egidio Meléndez
Spanish, 1716 – 1780,
Still Life with Grapes, Figs, and a Copper Kettle, c. 1770 – 80.

52.9.177 Luis Egidio Meléndez
Spanish, 1716 – 1780
Still Life with Game, c. 1770 – 80.

52.9.182 Bartolomé Pérez
Spanish, 1634 – 1693
A Vase of Flowers on a Table, c. 1660 – 70.

52.9.184 Juan Bautista Romero
Spanish, 1756 – after 1802
Still Life with Strawberries and Chocolate, c. 1770 – 90.

52.9.185 Juan Bautista Romero
Spanish, 1756 – after 1802
Still Life with Pastries, Wine, and Eggs, c. 1775 – 90.

52.9.186 Juan Bautista Romero
Spanish, 1756 – after 1802
Still Life with Flowers in a Vase, c. 1780 – 90.

52.9.187 Juan Bautista Romero
Spanish, 1756 – after 1802
Still Life with Flowers in a Basket, c. 1780 – 90.

52.9.188 Pedro de Camprobín
Spanish, 1605 – 74
Still Life on a Brown Table, c. 1660.

52.9.189 Pedro de Camprobín
Spanish, 1605 – 74
Still Life on a Gray Table, c. 1660.

52.9.227 Anonymous, 19th century artist
Spanish
A Vase of Flowers on a Pedestal, 19th century.

Works of Art Purchased with Funds from the $1 million State of North Carolina Appropriation and the North Carolina Art Society (Robert F. Phifer Bequest)

52.9.22 Homer Martin
American, 1836 – 1897
Salt Meadows.

52.9.35 After Aelbert Cuyp
Dutch, 1620 – 1691
The Travelers' Halt, 18th or 19th century copy of a 17th century work.

52.9.52 Attributed to Jacob Ochtervelt
Dutch, c.1635 – c. 1709
Cavaliers and Ladies at a Table, c. 1665.

52.9.70 Thomas Gainsborough
British, 1727 – 1788
Portrait of Ralph Bell, 1772 – 74.

52.9.71 Thomas Gainsborough
British, 1727 – 1788
Landscape with Three Donkeys, 1780.

52.9.75 John Hoppner
British, 1758 – 1810
Portrait of a Family, c. 1800.

52.9.80 George Morland
British, 1763 – 1804
The Death of the Fox.

52.9.81 Henry Raeburn
British, 1756 – 1823
Charles James Fox.

52.9.83 Joshua Reynolds
British, 1723 – 1792
Captain John Brice, 1764.

52.9.87 Attributed to Nathaniel Dance
British, 1735 – 1811
Oldfield Bowles (1740 – 1810), c. 1775 – 80.

52.9.101 Jacob Jordaens
Flemish, 1593 – 1678
The Holy Family, c. 1615.

52.9.109 Peter Paul Rubens and Cornelis de Vos
Flemish, 1577 – 1640 and 1585 – 1651
Philip III, 1635 – 40.

52.9.110 Peter Paul Rubens and Cornelis de Vos
Flemish, 1577 – 1640 and 1585 – 1651
Philip IV, 1635 – 40.

52.9.111 Workshop of Peter Paul Rubens
Flemish, 1577 – 1640
Joan of Arc, c. 1620.

52.9.119 François Boucher
French, 1703 – 1770
The Abduction of Europa, 1747 – 70.

52.9.141 George Pencz
German, 1500 – 1550
Portrait of Martin Luther, 1533.

52.9.144 Francesco Bassano the Younger,
Italian, c. 1549 – 1592
The Adoration of the Shepherds, c. 1585 – 90.

52.9.191 Circle of Juan de Borgoña
Spanish, 1470 – 1536
Crucifixion with the Virgin and Saints John the Evangelist, Peter and Paul, c. 1520 – 40.

52.9.194/A – B Unknown
British
Marble Top Table, c. 1740.

52.9.198 Antonius Gunther Gheringh
Flemish, active c. 1662 – 1668
Interior of a Church, c. 1660.

52.9.199 Henry Raeburn
British, 1756 – 1823
Lt. General Alexander Campbell.

52.9.200 Jan Wijk
British, 1640 – 1702
Deer Hunt, c. 1696.

Works of Art Given by William R. Valentiner

G.55.13.1 Díaz de la Peña
Spanish, 1807 – 1876
A Little Girl and Her Pet.

G.56.12.3 Thomas Sully
American, 1783 – 1872
Boy with a Cat.

G.57.34.2 Clayton S. Price
American, 1874 – 1950
Two Heads.

G.57.34.3 Richard Diebenkorn
American, 1922 – 1993
Berkeley No. 8, 1954.

G.57.34.11 Attributed to Tino di Camaino
Italian, 1285 – 1337
Madonna and Child.

Works of Art Acquired through the Bequest of William R. Valentiner

G.65.10.1 William Baziotes
American, 1912 – 1963
Moon Animal, 1949.

G.65.10.2 Max Beckmann
German, 1884 – 1950
Portrait of W. R. Valentiner, 1950.

G.65.10.3 Max Beckmann
German, 1884 – 1950
Footbridge over the River, c. 1922.

G.65.10.4 Max Beckmann
German, 1884 – 1950
Self Portrait.

G.65.10.5 Harry Bertoia
American, born Italy, 1915 – 1978
Sculpture.

G.65.10.6 Harry Bertoia
American, born Italy, 1915 – 1978
Landscape.

G.65.10.7 Harry Bertoia
American, born Italy, 1915 – 1978
Tree.

G.65.10.8 Attributed to Ferdinand Bol
Dutch, 1616 – 1680
Departure of Tobias.

G.65.10.9 Georges Braque
French, 1882 – 1963
Bird.

G.65.10.10 Lucile Brokaw
American, born 1915
Moon Lady, 1957.

G.65.10.11 Lovis Corinth
German, 1858 – 1925
Female Figure, 1918

G.65.10.12 Charles Demuth
American, 1883 – 1935
Flowers, c. 1915.

G.65.10.13 Charles Despiau
French, 1891 – 1946
Mask.

G.65.10.14 Richard Diebenkorn
American, 1922 – 1993
Untitled, 1951.

G.65.10.15 Attributed to Gerbrand van den
Eeckhout
Dutch, 1621 – 1674
Young Man Standing in Profile.

G.65.10.16 James Ensor
Belgian, 1860 – 1949
Masks, 1892.

G.65.10.17 Lyonel Feininger
American, (active in Germany
1887 – 1937), 1871 – 1956
The Green Bridge II (etching),
1910 – 11.

G.65.10.18 John Flannagan
American, 1895 – 1942
Bear.

G.65.10.19 Attributed to Govert Flinck
Dutch, 1615 – 1660
Standing Man.

G.65.10.20 Alberto Giacometti
Swiss, 1901 – 1966
Study for Sculpture, 1948.

G.65.10.21 Adolph Gottlieb
American, 1903 – 1974
Incubus, 1947.

G.65.10.22 Circle of Hendrick Goudt
Dutch, 1585 – 1630
Two Figures.

G.65.10.23 Morris Graves
American, born 1910
Raven in Moonlight, 1943.

G.65.10.24 Emilio Greco
Italian, born 1913
Pinocchio.

G.65.10.25/1-3 Emilio Greco
Italian, born 1913
Head of a Woman, 1951.

G.65.10.26 Erich Heckel
German, 1883 – 1970
Landscape, 1921.

G.65.10.27 Barbara Hepworth
British, 1903 – 1975
Curlew II-String, 1957.

G.65.10.28 Attributed to Samuel van
Hoogstraten
Dutch, 1627 – 1678
St. Peter Praying for Tabea.

G.65.10.29 Wassily Kandinsky
Russian, 1866 – 1944
Zunehmen, 1933.

G.65.10.30 Ernst Ludwig Kirchner
German, 1880 – 1938
Panama Girls, 1910.

G.65.10.31 Ernst Ludwig Kirchner
German, 1880 – 1938
Portrait of Ludwig Schames.

G.65.10.32 Ernst Ludwig Kirchner
German, 1880 – 1938
Still Life, Flowers, 1935.

G.65.10.33 Paul Klee
Swiss, 1879 – 1940
Cottage with Palms, 1925.

G.65.10.34/1-8 Oskar Kokoschka
Austrian, 1886 – 1980
Die Chinesische Mauer.

G.65.10.35/1-10 Oskar Kokoschka
Austrian, 1886 – 1980
Book of Original Lithographs.

G.65.10.36 Oskar Kokoschka
Austrian, 1886 – 1980
Princess Lichnowsky.

G.65.10.37 Oskar Kokoschka
Austrian, 1886 – 1980
Woman's Head.

G.65.10.38 Georg Kolbe
German, 1877 – 1947
Standing Figure, 1917 – 20.

G.65.10.39 Georg Kolbe
German, 1877 – 1947
Kneeling Figure, 1917 – 20.

G.65.10.40 Georg Kolbe
German, 1877 – 1947
Kneeling Figure.

G.65.10.41 Käthe Kollwitz
German, 1867 – 1945
*Self-Portrait with Hand to
Forehead.*

G.65.10.42 Wilhelm Lehmbruck
German, 1881 – 1919
Head of a Woman, 1913 – 14.

G.65.10.43 Nicolaes Maes
Dutch, 1634 – 1693
Three Orientals.

G.65.10.44 Aristide Maillol
French, 1861 – 1944
Study for Cézanne Monument.

G.65.10.45 Arturo Martini
Italian, 1889 – 1947
Three Graces in Landscape.

G.65.10.46 Claes Moeyaert
Dutch, 1592 – 1655
Christ Healing a Sick Woman.

G.65.10.47 Henry Moore
British, 1898 – 1986
Family Group (drawing).

G.65.10.48 Otto Mueller
German, 1874 – 1930
Two Nude Figures in a Landscape.

G.65.10.49 Otto Mueller
German, 1874 – 1930
Two Figures.

G.65.10.50 Emil Nolde
German, 1862 – 1956
Landscape, 1925.

G.65.10.51 Emil Nolde
German, 1862 – 1956
Still Life, Tulips, 1930.

G.65.10.52 Serge Poliakoff
French, 1906 – 1969
Composition, c. 1953.

G.65.10.53 Candido Portinari
Brazilian, born 1903
Woman and Cow, 1939.

G.65.10.54 Karl John Priebe
American, born 1914
Circus Trio, 1944.

G.65.10.55 Diego Rivera
Mexican, 1886 – 1957
Portrait of Dr. Valentiner, 1932.

G.65.10.56 Christian Rohlfs
German, 1849 – 1938
Still Life, c. 1938.

G.65.10.57 Richard Schiebe
German, 1889 – 1965
Medallion.

G.65.10.58 Karl Schmidt-Rottluff
German, 1884 – 1976
Portrait of Emy, 1919.

G.65.10.59 Karl Schmidt-Rottluff
German, 1884 – 1976
Still Life, 1922.

G.65.10.60 David Smith
American, 1906 – 1965
Classic Figure III, 1945.

G.65.10.61 Attributed to Frans Snyders
Flemish, 1579 – 1657
Deer Hunt.

G.65.10.62 Christoph Gertner
German, 1546 – 1611
Venus & Satyr.

G.65.10.63 Graham Sutherland
British, 1903 – 1980
Reclining Stone Form, 1948.

G.65.10.64 Diego Velásquez
Spanish, 1599 – 1660
Cavalier.

G.65.10.65 Jan Victors
Dutch
Angel Appearing to Manoah,
1620.

G.65.10.66 Theodor Werner
German, 1886 – 1969
Abstract.

G.65.10.67 Fritz Winter
German, 1905 – 1976
Unfolding, 1949.

G.65.10.68 Emerson Woelffer
American, born 1914
Untitled 1953, 1953.

G.65.10.69 Gerhard Marcks
German, 1889 – 1964
Medallion of Heinrich Wölfflin.

G.65.10.70 Unknown
Coptic
Fabric.

G.65.10.71 Unknown
S. German
Madonna as Queen of Heaven,
18th century.

G.65.10.72/1-20 Willi Baumeister
German, 1889 – 1955
Sport und Maschine, 1929.

G.65.10.73 Alfred Kubin
German, 1877 – 1959
Ein Totentanz.

G.65.10.74/1–8 George Schrimpf
German, 1883 – 1938
Acht Holschnitte, 1916.

G.65.10.75 Georg Kolbe
German, 1877 – 1947
Female Figure.

G.65.10.76 Pierantonio Novelli
Italian, 1728 – 1804
Drawing.

G.65.10.77 Fernando Puma
American, 1915 – 1957
Dancing Horse.

G.65.10.78 Chaim Gross
American, 1904 – 1991
Two Figures, 1949.

G.65.10.79 Mabelle Richardson
American, 1908 – 1965
Seated Figure.

G.65.10.80 Lillian Freiman
Canadian, 1908 – 1965
Woman Peeling Potatoes.

G.65.10.81 Lillian Freiman
Canadian, 1908 – 1965
Woman Holding Bird.

G.65.10.82 John Carroll
American, 1892 – 1957
The Tumblers.

G.65.10.83 Oskar Kokoschka
Austrian, 1886 – 1980
Die Traumenden Knaben, 1917.

G.65.10.84 Oskar Kokoschka
Austrian, 1886 – 1980
Der Gefesselte Columbus, 1921.

G.65.10.85 Otto Mueller
German, 1874 – 1930
Head of a Man.

Works of Art Given by the Samuel H. Kress Foundation

GL.60.17.1 Segna di Bonaventura
Italian, 1298 – c. 1331
Madonna and Child, c. 1320 – 30.

GL.60.17.2 Attributed to Niccolò di Segna
Italian, active c. 1330 – 1350
Christ Blessing, c. 1340 – 50.

GL.60.17.3 Attributed to the Master
of San Torpé
Italian, active c. 1290 – 1320
*Madonna and Child with St.
Bartholomew and St. John the
Baptist*, c. 1315 – 20.

GL.60.17.4 Tino di Camaino
Italian, 1285 – 1337
Madonna and Child.

GL.60.17.5 Luca di Tommè
Italian, active 1356 – c. 1390
Christ Blessing, 1362 – 65.

GL.60.17.6 Follower of Pietro Lorenzetti
Italian, c. 1306 – 1348
*Madonna and Child, the
Crucifixion and Saints*,
c. 1340–70.

GL.60.17.7 Giotto di Bondone and
Assistants
Italian, c. 1266/76 – 1337
The "Peruzzi Altarpiece",
c. 1310 – 15.

GL.60.17.8 Puccio Capanna
Italian, active c. 1325 – 1350
The Crucifixion, c. 1330.

GL.60.17.9 Master of the Rinuccini Chapel
Italian, active c. 1350 – 75
St. Cosmas and St. Damian,
c. 1370 – 75.

GL.60.17.10 Mariotto di Nardo
Italian, documented 1393 – 1424
*Crucifixion with St. John the
Baptist, the Virgin, St. John the
Evangelist, and St. Nicholas*,
c. 1385 – 90.

GL.60.17.11 Pseudo Jacopino di Francesco
Italian, active c. 1320 – 1350
*The Nativity and the Adoration
of the Magi*, c. 1325 – 30.

GL.60.17.12 Pseudo Jacopino di Francesco
Italian, active c. 1320 – 1350
*St. Mary Magdalene Washing
Christ's Feet*, c. 1325 – 30.

GL.60.17.13 Pseudo Jacopino di Francesco
Italian, active c. 1320 – 1350
*St. John the Evangelist Restoring
Two Men to Life*, c. 1325 – 30.

GL.60.17.14 Pseudo Jacopino di Francesco
Italian, active c. 1320 – 1350
*St. Catherine of Alexandria Freed
from the Wheel*, c. 1325 – 30.

GL.60.17.15 Pseudo Jacopino di Francesco
Italian, active c. 1320 – 1350
*The Beheading of St. Catherine of
Alexandria*, c. 1325 – 30.

GL.60.17.16 Attributed to the Master of San
Jacopo a Mucciana
Italian, active late 14th century
St. Jerome in His Study,
c. 1390 – 1400.

GL.60.17.17 Guariento d'Arpo
Italian, active 1338 – 1368/70
Madonna and Child with Saints,
c. 1360.

GL.60.17.18 Attributed to Francescuccio
Ghissi
Italian, active from c. 1359 – 1395
*St. John the Evangelist Reproving
the Philosopher Crato*,
c. 1370 – 80.

GL.60.17.19 Attributed to Francescuccio
Ghissi
Italian, active from c. 1359 – 1395
*Acteus and Eugenius Imploring
St. John the Evangelist to Restore
Their Wealth*, c. 1370 – 80.

GL.60.17.20 Attributed to Francescuccio
Ghissi
Italian, active from 1359 – 1395
*St. John the Evangelist and the
Poisoned Cup*, c. 1370 – 80.

GL.60.17.21 Pavian School
Italian
*Madonna and Child with St. John
the Evangelist, a Donor, and St.
Anthony Abbot*, c. 1400.

GL.60.17.22 Vincenzo Foppa
Italian, 1427/30 – 1515/16
Madonna and Child, c. 1460 – 70.

GL.60.17.23 Workshop of Apollonio di
Giovanni
Italian, 1415/17 – 1465
The Triumph of Chastity,
c. 1450 – 60.

GL.60.17.24 Attribut ed to Paolo Uccello
Italian, 1397 – 1475
Madonna and Child, c. 1430 – 35.

GL.60.17.25 Francesco di Simone Ferrucci
Italian, 1437 – 1493
Madonna and Child, c. 1480.

GL.60.17.26 Sandro Botticelli, and Assistants
Italian, 1444/5 – 1510
The Adoration of the Child,
c. 1500.

GL.60.17.27 Workshop of Filippino Lippi
Italian, 1457 – 1504
St. Donatus, c. 1495 – 96.

GL.60.17.28 Workshop of Filippino Lippi
Italian, 1457 – 1504
St. Augustine, c. 1495 – 96.

GL.60.17.29 Neroccio de' Landi and
Workshop
Italian, 1447 – 1500
Visit of Cleopatra to Antony,
c. 1475 – 80.

GL.60.17.30 Neroccio de' Landi and
Workshop
Italian, 1447 – 1500
The Battle of Actium, c. 1475 – 80.

GL.60.17.31 Benvenuto di Giovanni
Italian, c. 1436 – 1518
*St. John Gualbert and the
Crucifix*, c. 1470.

GL.60.17.32 Follower of Giovanni Antonio
Bazzi, called Il Sodoma
Italian, 1477 – 1549
Leda and the Swan, c. 1565 – 75.

GL.60.17.33 Workshop of Pietro Perugino
Italian, c. 1450 – 1523
The Mourning Virgin, c. 1520.

GL.60.17.34 Workshop of Pietro Perugino
Italian, c. 1450 – 1523
*The Mourning St. John the
Evangelist,* c. 1520.

GL.60.17.35 Attributed to Bernardino
Pintoricchio
Italian, c.1454 – 1513
Madonna and Child,
c. 1495 – 1500.

GL.60.17.36 Lorenzo Costa
Italian, 1460 – 1535
The Miracle of the Catafalque,
(Panel A), c. 1490 – 95.

GL.60.17.37 Lorenzo Costa
Italian, 1460 – 1535
The Miracle of the Catafalque,
(Panel B), c. 1490 – 95.

GL.60.37.38 Lorenzo Costa
Italian, 1460 – 1535
The Miracle of the Catafalque,
(Panel C), c. 1490 – 95.

GL.60.17.39 Francesco Francia
Italian, c. 1450 – 1517/18
*Madonna and Child with Two
Angels,* c. 1495 – 1500.

GL.60.17.40 Giovanni Antonio Boltraffio
Italian, 1467 – 1516
*Portrait of a Girl Crowned with
Flowers,* c. 1490.

GL.60.17.41 Attributed to Titian
Italian, 1488/90 – 1576
The Adoration of the Child,
c. 1507 – 08.

GL.60.17.42 Workshop of Lorenzo Lotto
Italian, c. 1480 – 1556/57
*The Body of Christ Supported by
Angels,* c. 1513 – 16.

GL.60.17.43 Giovanni Antonio de' Sacchis,
called Il Pordenone
Italian, 1483/84 – 1539
St. Prosdocimus and St. Peter,
c. 1515 – 17.

GL.60.17.44 Giovanni Cariani
Italian, c. 1485 – after 1547
*Portrait of a Gentleman Wearing
a Gold Chain,* c. 1525 – 30.

GL.60.17.45 Bernardino Lanino
Italian, c. 1512 – 1583
*Madonna and Child Enthroned
with Saints and Donors,* 1552.

GL.60.17.46 Follower of Giovanni
Battista Moroni
Italian, 1520/24 – 1578
Portrait of a Man in Armor,
c. 1563.

GL.60.17.47 Veronese (Paolo Caliari)
Italian, 1528 – 1588
The Baptism of Christ,
c. 1550 – 60.

GL.60.17.48 Venetian School
Italian
Portrait of a Lady, c. 1570 – 80.

GL.60.17.49 Tintoretto (Jacopo Robusti)
Italian, 1560 – 1635
The Raising of Lazarus,
c. 1585 – 90.

GL.60.17.50 Franceso Bassano the Younger
(Francesco da Ponte) with
Jacopo Bassano (Jacopo da
Ponte), Italian, 1549 – 1592
and c. 1510 – 1592
The Scourging of Christ,
c. 1580 – 85.

GL.60.17.51 Domenichino
Italian, 1581 – 1641
*The Madonna of Loreto
Appearing to St. John the Baptist,
St. Eligius, and St. Anthony Abbot,*
1618 – 20.

GL.60.17.52 Massimo Stanzione
Italian, 1585 – 1656
The Assumption of the Virgin,
c. 1630 – 35.

GL.60.17.53 Giuseppe Ghislandi, called Fra
Vittore and Fra Galgario
Italian, 1655 – 1743
*Portrait of a Young Man as a
Gentleman,* c. 1720 – 30.

GL.60.17.54 Giuseppe Ghislandi, called Fra
Vittore and Fra Galgario
Italian, 1655 – 1743
*Portrait of a Young Man with a
Turban,* c. 1720 – 30.

GL.60.17.55 Giacomo Ceruti
Italian, 1698 – 1767
The Card Game, c. 1738 – 50.

GL.60.17.56 Alessandro Magnasco
Italian, 1667 – 1749
*The Supper of Pulcinella and
Colombina,* c. 1725 – 30.

GL.60.17.57 Alessandro Magnasco
Italian, 1667 – 1749
Bay with Shipwreck, c. 1710 – 20.

GL.60.17.58 Attributed to Antonio Marinetti
Italian, 1719 – 1796
*The Archangel Raphael with
Tobias,* c. 1760.

GL.60.17.59 Michele Marieschi
Italian, 1710 – 1743
*The Grand Canal at Palazzo
Foscari,* c. 1740.

GL.60.17.60 Pompeo Girolamo Batoni
Italian, 1708 – 1787
The Triumph of Venice, 1737.

GL.60.17.61 Master of the Latour D'Auvergne
Triptych
French, active c. 1490 – 1508
*The Annunciation with Saints
and Donors,* c. 1497.

GL.60.17.62 Attributed to Quentin Massys
Flemish, 1465 – 1530
Salvator Mundi, c. 1500 – 10.

GL.60.17.63 Circle of Hans Pleydenwurff
German, 1420 – 1472
St. Leonard, c. 1420 – 72.

GL.60.17.64 Style of Georg Breu, the Elder
German, 1475 – 1537
St. George and the Dragon,
c. 1520.

GL.60.17.65 Lucas Cranach, the Younger
German, 1515 – 1586
*Martin Luther and Philipp
Melanchthon,* 1558.

GL.60.17.66 Hendrick Ter Brugghen
Dutch, 1588 – 1629
*David Praised by the Israelite
Women,* 1623.

GL.60.17.67 Style of Frans Hals
Dutch, c. 1582/83 – 1666
A Fisherboy, c. 17th century.

GL.60.17.68 Attributed to Govert Flinck
Dutch, 1615 – 1660
A Young Man with a Sword,
c. 1633 – 36.

GL. 60.17.69 Gerrit Adriaensz. Berckheyde
Dutch, 1638 – 1698
*The Fish Market and the Grote
Kerk at Haarlem,* c. 1675 – 1680.

GL.60.17.70 Jan Siberechts
Flemish, 1627 – c. 1703
Pastoral Scene, c. 1665 – 70.

GL.60.17.71 Manner of Lorenzo Lotto
Italian, c. 1480 – 1556/57
The Martyrdom of St. Alexander.

The Kress Indenture
INDENTURE:

An agreement between the Samuel H. Kress Foundation and the State of North Carolina

THIS INDENTURE made as of the 9th day of December, 1961, between SAMUEL H. KRESS FOUNDATION, a non-profit corporation incorporated by a Special Act of the Legislature of the State of New York, having its principal office at 221 West 57th Street, New York 19, New York (hereinafter called the "DONOR"), and STATE OF NORTH CAROLINA (hereinafter called the "DONEE").
WITNESSETH, that the DONOR hereby grants and conveys to the DONEE the objects of art listed in the schedule annexed hereto and made a part hereof, TO HAVE AND TO HOLD in trust upon the following terms and conditions, which shall apply not only to the objects of art so listed but also to all objects of art hereafter donated by the DONOR to the DONEE:

1. The DONEE shall establish and maintain said objects of art, in good condition and under conditions suitable for their adequate protection and safety, exclusively for public, charitable and educational purposes, as, or as part of a permanent art exhibit in the North Carolina Art Museum in the City of Raleigh, North Carolina, or in such other museum in said city as may be used by the DONEE as its principal art museum.

2. The DONEE shall permanently display said objects of art as a unified collection, suitably identified as "The Samuel H. Kress collection", in a manner suitable for objects of art of their character and quality.

3. The DONEE shall permanently maintain on each of said objects of art the name-plate attached thereto at the time of the delivery thereof, or a duplicate of such a name-plate.

4. The DONEE shall not cause or permit any of said objects of art to be reproduced or publicized without being accredited in each instance to "The Samuel H. Kress Collection" and to the museum in which they are displayed by the DONEE.

5. Compliance with any term or condition herein above set forth in any particular instance may be excused by the DONOR by written waiver which shall specifically identify the term or condition compliance with which is waived and specify the act or condition of non-compliance to which the waiver applies.

6. If at any time the DONEE shall cease to exist, or shall fail to comply with any of the terms or conditions set forth in paragraphs 1 and 2 hereof without having obtained a waiver of compliance pursuant to paragraph 5 hereof, the title to and right to possession of all of said objects of art shall revert to and vest in, and said objects of art shall be delivered to, the DONOR, its successors and assigns.

IN WITNESS WHEREOF, the parties have caused this Indenture to be executed in their respective corporate names by their respective officers or other persons thereunto duly authorized and their respective corporate seals to be hereunto affixed and attested, as of the day and year first above written.

SAMUEL H. KRESS FOUNDATION
By (Franklin D. Murphy) Vice President
(R. H. Kress) President
(Guy Emerson) Art Director
Attest: (F.C. Geiger) Secretary

STATE OF NORTH CAROLINA
By (Terry Sanford) Governor
Attest: (Thad Eure) Secretary of State

Works of Art Given by Mr. and Mrs. Gordon Hanes

G.72.3.1 Unknown
Egyptian
Vase, black-top ware, Early
Predynastic, 4000 – 3500 B. C.

GL.72.19.3 Senufo Tribe
African
Society banner, 20th century.

GL.72.19.4 Yoruba Tribe
African
Shango staff, 20th century.

GL.72.19.6 Baule Tribe
African
Bush cow helmet mask crest,
20th century.

GL.72.19.7 Bakuba Tribe
African
Male head, 20th century.

GL.72.19.8 Bakuba Tribe
African
Cup, male head, western handle,
20th century.

GL.72.19.9 Lega Tribe
African
Bwami Society figure, (Iginga),
20th century.

GL.72.19.10 Lega Tribe
African
Bwami figure, 20th century.

GL.72.19.11 Lega Tribe
African
Bwami figure, 20th century.

GL.72.19.13 Bajokwe Tribe
African
Hunter's whistle, 20th century.

GL.72.19.14 Baule Tribe
African
Gong striker, 20th century.

GL.72.19.15 Bambara Tribe
African
Bowl with janus figure crest,
20th century.

GL.72.19.17 Ashanti Tribe
African
Ritual vessel, 20th century.

GL.72.19.18 Zuñi Tribe
African
War god figure.

GL.72.19.23 Zulu Tribe
African
Single headrest/stool,
20th century.

GL.72.19.28 Baule Tribe
African
Dance mask with horns,
20th century.

GL.72.19.34 Yoruba Tribe
African
Smith's staff, 20th century.

GL.72.19.36 M'Pongwe Tribe
African
Helmet mask, 20th century.

GL.72.19.38 Baluba Tribe
African
Bowl bearer, (Mboko),
20th century.

GL.72.19.41 Bakota Tribe
African
Reliquary guardian figure,
20th century.

GL.72.19.42 Ashanti Tribe
African
Fertility doll, (Akuaba),
20th century.

GL.72.19.43 Benin Tribe
African
Staff, (Ahianwen-oro),
20th century.

GL.72.19.46 Gurunsi Tribe
African
Hornbill mask, 20th century.

GL.72.19.47 Senufo Tribe
African
House door, 20th century.

GL.72.19.48 Yoruba Tribe
African
Divination tray, Eshu head,
20th century.

74.1.32 John Taylor Arms
American, 1887 – 1953
Black Rock.

SC.74.2.1 Unknown
European
*Textile, brocaded panel with
silver bullion.*

SC.74.2.2 Unknown
Flemish
Textile, border from a hanging,
17th century.

SC.74.2.3 Unknown
Far Eastern
Textile, medallion, 19th century.

SC.74.2.4 Unknown
European
Textile panel.

G.74.19.1 Unknown
Greek, Mycenean
Roman Goddess, Late Helladic III,
1400 – 1150 B. C.

G.74.19.2 Unknown
Greek, Mycenean
Woman holding a child,
Late Helladic III, 1400 – 1150 B. C.

G.74.19.3 Unknown
Cypriot
Idol, Early Bronze Age, 2000 B. C.

G.74.19.4 Unknown
Egyptian
*Shawabti Box with Two Shawabti
Figures,* New Kingdom, Dynasty
XX (1197 – 1085 B. C.).

G.74.19.5 Unknown
Etruscan
Footed jar, 7th century B. C.

G.74.19.6 Unknown
Etruscan
Mirror, showing Hermes & Paris,
c. 300 B. C.

G.74.19.7 Unknown
New Guinean
Trophy head.

G.74.19.8 Unknown
Egyptian
Stylized figure.

GL.75.5.1 Maurice Vlaminck
French, 1876 – 1958
Vase of Flowers.

G.75.8.1 Henry Moore
British, 1898 – 1986
*Seated Figures & Ideas for
Sculpture,* 1973.

G.75.8.2 Giovanni Battista Piranesi
Italian,
*The Piazza del Quirinale with the
Statues of the Horsetamers Seen
from the Back,* 1773.

G.75.8.3 Unknown
Greek, Attic
Column Krater, Early 5th century.

G.75.8.4 Unknown
Egyptian
Reclining Bull, 600 – 400 B. C.

G.75.8.5 Paul Hartley
American, born 1943
Courtyard, 1974.

G.75.8.6 Claude Flynn Howell
American, 1915 – 1997
Unloading Fish, 1974.

G.75.8.7 Claude Flynn Howell
American, 1915 – 1997
Mending Nets, 1974.

G.75.8.8 Claude Flynn Howell
American, 1915 – 1997
Nets and Decoys, 1974.

G.76.7.1 Matthew K. Smartt
American, born 1954
Baby Rhinoceros, 1975.

G.76.7.2 Bamileke Tribe
African
Pipe, 20th century.

G.76.7.3 Marvin Saltzman
American, born 1931
Pawleys Island, 1973.

SC.77.2.1 Unknown
New Guinean
Lime container.

SC.77.2.2 Unknown
New Guinean
Head.

SC.77.2.3 Unknown
New Guinean
Head.

G.77.2.1 Frederick William Macmonnies
American, 1863 – 1937
Bacchante, 1893.

G.77.2.2 Sheila Bocock
American, born 1915
No Beach Today.

G.77.2.3 Harry Bertoia
American, born Italy, 1915 – 1978
Gong Structure.

G.77.2.4 Bernard Baschet
French, 1917 – 1977
Couple II.

G.77.2.5 Unknown
New Guinean
Dagger.

G.77.2.6 Unknown
Prince Alexander Region, Boiken
Bride wealth mask, 20th century.

G.77.2.7 Unknown
Peruvian
Bowl.

G.77.2.8 Matthew K. Smartt
American, born 1948
In Search of the Deja.

G.77.2.9 Michael Ehlbeck
American, born 1948
Cow.

G.77.2.10 Yoruba Tribe
African
Headdress, 20th century.

G.77.2.11 Unknown
Flemish
Crucifix figure, 17th century.

G.77.2.12 Unknown
Dutch
Covered goblet, c. 1719.

G.77.2.13 Unknown
Dutch
Covered goblet, c. 1719.

G.77.2.14 Unknown
Dutch
Goblet with Coat of Arms, c. 1778.

G.77.2.16 Unknown
Chinese
Textile, hanging in five sections.

GL.78.6.1 Kenneth Noland
American, born 1924
Greek Vision, 1970.

G.78.6.2 John James Audubon
American, 1785 – 1851
Florida Jay.

G.78.6.3 George Luks
American, 1867 – 1933
The White Cat, 1930.

G.78.6.4 Saliba Douaihy
American, born 1915
Seascape, 1950.

G.78.6.5 Saliba Douaihy
American, born 1915
Mediterranean, 1960.

G.78.6.6 Saliba Douaihy
American, born 1915
Regeneration, 1974.

G.79.6.1 Haida Tribe
North American
Totem pole, 20th century.

G.79.6.2 John James Audubon
American, 1785 – 1851
Mallard Duck.

G.79.6.3 Unknown
Egyptian
Striding Man, Old Kingdom,
Dynasty V, c. 2490 – 2180 B. C.

G.79.6.4 Unknown
Egyptian
Frog, 1st/2nd Dynasty,
2955 – 2635 B. C.

SC.79.6.5 Unknown
Mycenean
Bull, c. 1400 – 1200 B. C.

G.79.6.6 Unknown
Greek
Skyphos, c. 400 – 350 B. C.

G.79.6.7 Unknown
Roman
Buff clay lamp, 1st century A. D.

G.79.6.8 Unknown
Roman, North African
Red clay lamp,
4th – 5th century A. D.

G.79.6.9 Unknown
Roman
Mosaic, c. 2nd century A. D.

G.79.6.10 Unknown
Chinese
Shan drum,
Late 18th-early 19th century.

G.79.6.11 Jean-Antoine Houdon
French, 1741 – 1828
Bust of Madame de Grandmenil.

G.79.6.12 Unknown
Cypriot
Head of a god or priest.

G.79.6.13 Unknown
Roman
*Funerary Stele of the Priest
Dionysios and his wife, Tertia*,
3rd century A. D.

G.79.6.14 Thomas Lawrence
British, 1769 – 1830
Head of a Girl.

G.79.6.15 Attributed to Tatillon Painter
Greek
Hydria, End of 3rd century B. C.

G.79.6.16 Jim Dine
American, born 1935
Bananas, 1972.

G.79.6.17 Jasper Johns
American, born 1930
Torso, 1974.

G.79.6.18 Roy Lichtenstein
American, born 1923
Guggenheim Poster, c. 1969.

G.79.6.19 Robert Rauschenberg
American, born 1925
Veils 3, c. 1974.

G79.6.20 Andy Warhol
American, 1928 – 1987
Black Drag Queen, c. 1975.

G.79.6.21 Karl Prantl
American, born 1923
Meditation Stone, 1977.

G.79.6.22 Masayuki Nagare
Japanese, born 1923
Ibachi Na-S2, 1977.

G.79.6.23/1–3 Pierre Alechinsky
Belgian, born 1927
Untitled, 1977.

G.79.6.24 Sheila Isham
American, 1927 – 1979
Cheth, August 1972, 1972.

G.79.6.25 Sheila Isham
American, 1927 – 1979
#77 Haiti, Mystical Space Dream.

G.79.6.26 Chryssa
American, born Greece, 1933
Untitled, c. 1965.

G.79.11.5 Painter of the Brussels
Oinochoai
Greek
Oinochoe, 470 – 460 B. C.

G.79.11.6 Unknown
Greek, Attic
Amphoriscos, 4th century B. C.

G.79.11.8 Unknown
Roman
Sarcophagus fragment,
c. 3rd century A. D.

G.80.6.1 Unknown
Polish
Torah crown, 19th century.

G.80.6.2 Unknown
Thai
Housepost, 20th century.

G.80.6.3 Henry Spencer Moore
British, 1898 – 1986
Large Spindle Piece, 1974.

G.80.6.4 Unknown
Greek, S. Italy
Guttus, 4th century B. C.

82.11 Unknown
Egyptian
Bust of the Goddess Sekhmet,
New Kingdom, 18th Dynasty,
c. 1570 – 1340 B. C.

82.12 Unknown
Egyptian
Model Boat, Middle Kingdom,
12th – 13th Dynasty,
2052 – 1178 B. C.

82.13 Unknown
Egyptian
Jar, 300 B.C.

82.14 Unknown
New World, Chiapas
Ball Court Marker, 600 – 900 A.D.

82.15 Morris Louis
American, 1912 – 1962
Pi, 1960.

82.16 Frank Stella
American, born 1936
Raqqa II, 1970.

82.17 Robert Allen Nelson
American, born 1925
The Pushover, 1981.

82.18 Thomas Downing
American, born 1928
Plumb Blue, 1963.

86.4 Unknown
Roman
Torso of an Emperor in the Guise of Jupiter, c. 1st century A.D.

86.5 Steiner Master
Cycladic
Female Figurine, Early Cycladic, c. 2500 – 2400 B.C.

86.6 Polychrome Group
Villanovan or Early Etruscan
Neck-Amphora, early 6th century B.C.

86.7 Unknown
Urn, 700 – 900 A.D.

86.8 Veracruz
Mexican
Priestess, 500 – 900 A.D.

86.9 Unknown
Melanesian
Helmet mask, 20th century.

86.10 Unknown
Melanesian
Bark belt with relief carvings of human faces, 20th century.

86.11 Unknown
Micronesian
Coconut grater, 20th century.

86.12 Sepik River People
Melanesian
Kandimbing, 20th century.

86.13 Unknown
Melanesian
Mask, 20th century.

86.14 Unknown
Melanesian
Slit gong, 20th century.

86.15 Maori
New Zealand
Wahaika, 19th century.

86.16 Unknown
Melanesian
Tapa cloth.

86.17 Unknown
Melanesian
Mask, 20th century.

86.18 Unknown
Melanesian
Ceremonial adze and stand, 20th century.

86.19 Unknown
Melanesian
Double hook.

86.20 Lower Sepik River People
Melanesian
Neckrest, 20th century.

86.25 Unknown
Peruvian
Tapestry depicting three warriors holding trophy heads, 14th century.

86.26 Unknown
Peruvian
Tapestry with checkerboard and birds, 1100 – 1532.

91.5 Unknown
Greek
Lekythos showing two figures with greek inscription above, 375 – 350 B.C.

91.6 Unknown
Egyptian
Anubis in the Form of a Reclining Jackal, 400 – 300 B.C.

91.7 Unknown
African
Oath-taking and healing image, (Nkondi).

92.1 Unknown
Roman
Portrait of the Emperor Marcus Aurelius, c. 190 A.D. With Mrs. Chauncey McCormick, by exchange.

Works of Art given by the Hanes Corporation

GL.72.19.1 Yoruba Tribe
African
Helmet mask, 20th century.

GL.72.19.2 Toma Tribe
African
Mask, 20th century.

GL.72.19.5 Basonge Tribe
African
Standing fetish figure (male), 20th century.

GL.72.19.12 Senufo Tribe
African
Poro Society mask (Kpelie), 20th century.

GL.72.19.16 M'Pongwe Tribe
African
Mask with bird crest, 20th century.

GL.72.19.19 Dan Tribe
African
Poro Society mask, 20th century.

GL.72.19.20 Bapende Tribe
African
Mbuya initiation mask, 20th century.

GL.72.19.21 Guro Tribe
African
Face mask with leopard crest, 20th century.

GL.72.19.22 Eskimo
Canadian
Mask.

GL.72.19.24 Bajokwe Tribe
African
Stool supported by standing woman and child, 20th century.

GL.72.19.25 Guro Tribe
African
Mask with unusual dual horn sets, 20th century.

GL.72.19.26 Ekoi Tribe
African
Mask headdress, 20th century.

GL.72.19.27 Vai Tribe
African
Helmet mask with face mask, 20th century.

GL.72.19.29 Dogon Tribe
African
Mask, 20th century.

GL.72.19.30 Dan-N'Guere Tribe
African
Face mask, 20th century.

GL.72.19.31 Ibo Tribe
African
Animal spirit, 20th century.

GL.72.19.32 Mano Tribe
African
Mask (Poro Society), 20th century.

GL.72.19.33 Baga Tribe
African
Ancestral shrine (Elek), 20th century.

GL.72.19.35 Bwa Tribe
African
Bush cow mask, 20th century.

GL.72.19.37 Bamana Tribe
African
Antelope headpiece (Tji Wara), 20th century.

GL.72.19.39 Bambara Tribe
African
Antelope headpiece, 20th century.

GL.72.19.40 Dogon Tribe
African
Mask, 20th century.

GL.72.19.44 Bambara Tribe
African
Mask (Boy's Initiation),
20th century.

GL.72.19.45 Senufo Tribe
African
*Helmet mask, (Waniugo/
Kponiugo)*, 20th century.

G.77.15.1 Unknown
Iraqi
Eternal Light (Ner Tamid),
18th century.

G.77.15.2 Unknown
German?
*Burial Society Cup Depicting Two
Scenes From the Life of Moses*,
c. 1895.

Works of Art Given by the James G. Hanes Memorial Fund

G.68.18.1 Thomas Sully
American, 1783 – 1872
*Udney Maria Blakeley
(1815 – 1842)*, 1830. With Dr. Edgar
D. Baker and Dr. G. Fred Hale.

G.72.2.1 Unknown
Egyptian
*Relief from the Tomb of Khnumti
in Saqqarah*, 2420 – 2258 B. C.

G.72.2.2 Unknown
Egyptian
*Relief from the Tomb of Khnumti
in Saqqarah*, 2420 – 2258 B. C.

G.72.2.3 Unknown
Egyptian
Corner Relief with Offering Scene,
285 – 246 B. C.

G.72.2.4 Bini Tribe
African
Shrine of the Hand (ikegobo),
before 1897.

G.73.8.1 Unknown
Egyptian
Mummy Mask, 1200 – 1080 B. C.

G.73.8.2 Unknown
Egyptian
Comb, after 1554 B. C.

G.73.8.3 Unknown
Japanese
Haniwa.

G.73.8.4 Unknown
Egyptian
*Mummy Case of Djed Mout
(Female)*, 945 – 712 B. C.

G.73.8.5 Unknown
Egyptian
Mummy Case of Amonred (Male),
945 – 712 B. C.

G.73.8.6 Unknown
Egyptian
Jar, 4000 – 3200 B. C.

G.73.8.7 Unknown
Egyptian
Jar, 3600 – 3200 B. C.

G.73.8.8 Unknown
Egyptian
Ointment jar, 1570 – 1314 B. C.

G.73.8.9 Unknown
Egyptian
Bowl, 663 – 525 B. C.

G.73.8.10 Unknown
Egyptian
Jar-vase, 400 – 300 B. C.

G.73.8.11 Unknown
Peruvian
Double spouted vessel.

G.73.8.12 Maya
Guatemalan
Jar, 500 – 700 A. D.

G.73.8.13 Mitsogo Tribe
African
Staff end.

G.73.8.14 Baule Tribe
African
Mask for the Goli dance.

G.73.8.15 Unknown
African
Bronze bell, 19th century.

G.73.8.16 Eskimo
Alaskan
Fish jawbone, 19th century.

G.73.8.17 Eskimo
Alaskan
Fish jawbone, 19th century.

G.73.8.18 Eskimo
Alaskan
Large fish jawbone, 19th century.

G.73.8.19 Eskimo
Alaskan
Oval mask.

G.73.8.20 Salish Tribe
North American
Mask, c. 1880.

G.73.8.21 Eskimo
Alaskan
Mask, 19th century.

G.73.8.22 New Ireland People
Melanesian
Helmet mask, 20th century.

G.73.8.23 Eskimo
Alaskan
Wood Mask, early 20th century

G.73.8.24 Zuñi Tribe
North American
Leather mask.

G.73.8.25 Mende Tribe
African
Sande Society mask (Bondo),
20th century.

G.73.8.26 Bayaka Tribe
African
Fetish figure.

G.73.8.27 Bapende Tribe
African
Helmet mask.

G.73.8.28 Bakuba Tribe
African
Box with lid.

G.73.8.29 Bakuba Tribe
African
Cosmetic box (Ngedi Mu Ntey),
19th century.

G.73.8.30/1-7 Ashanti Tribe
African
Goldweights.

G.78.3.31 Unknown
New Guinean
Housepost.

G.78.3.32 Unknown
New Guinean
Dance helmet mask.

G.73.8.33 Unknown
New Guinean
Sago bowl.

G.73.8.34 Unknown
New Guinean
Sago bowl.

G.73.8.35 Unknown
New Guinean
Figure.

G.73.8.36 Unknown
New Guinean
House mask.

G.73.8.37 Unknown
New Guinean
Drum.

G.73.8.38 Unknown
Mexican, Nayarit
Female figure, Classic Period,
c. 500 B.C. – 1000 A. D.

G.73.8.39 Colima
Mexican
Kneeling figure, Pre-Classic
Period, c. 200 B. C. – 300 A. D.

SC.74.1.1 Unknown
Byzantine footed bowl,
5th century.

G.74.2.1 Unknown
New Guinean
Ancestral figure.

G.74.2.2 Unknown
New Ireland
Head.

G.74.2.3 Unknown
New Ireland
Sculpture fragment.

G.74.2.4 Unknown
Melanesian
Dance wand.

G.74.2.5   Unknown
Canaanite
Standing figure, 3200 – 2100 B. C.

G.74.2.6   Unknown
Canaanite
Standing figure, 3200 – 2100 B. C.

G.74.2.7   Unknown
Egyptian
Royal Portrait head,
1570 – 1349 B. C.

G.74.2.8   Unknown
Egyptian
*Head from a Shawabti figure of
Akhenaten*, 1372 – 1355 B. C.

G.74.2.9   Unknown
Egyptian
*Mummiform Coffin with Head of
Horus*, 600 – 400 B. C.

G.74.2.10   Unknown
Mexican
Standing "smiling" figure.

G.74.2.11   Mochica
Peruvian
Stirrup spout vessel,
200 – 500 A. D.

G.74.2.12   Unknown
Colombian
Cylindrical vessel,
c. 1000 – 1500 A. D.

G.74.2.13   Unknown
Mexican
Tripod vessel, 300 – 600 A. D.

G.74.2.14   Baule Tribe
African
Mask.

G.74.2.15   Unknown
New Guinean
Lime container with bird stopper.

G.74.2.16   Unknown
Melanesian
Lime spatula.

G.74.2.17   Unknown
New Guinean
Suspension hook.

G.74.2.18   Unknown
Melanesian
Suspension hook.

G.74.2.19   Unknown
Melanesian
Dagger, 20th century.

G.74.2.20   Unknown
New Zealand
Bird snare fragment,
20th century.

SC.74.2.29   Daniel Hoffer
German, 1470 – 1536
Fête de Village.

SC.74.2.30   Melchior Meier
Swiss, 16th century
Flaying of Marsyas, c. 1582.

SC.74.2.31   Heinrich Aldegrever
German, 1502 – c. 1558
Lot Welcomes the Angels, 1555.

SC.74.2.32   Marc Raimondi
Italian, 1480 – 1527
Satyr et L'Enfant.

Works of Art Purchased with Funds from the North Carolina Art Society (Robert F. Phifer Bequest)

46.1.1   Kenneth Evett
American, born 1913
The Carpenter, c. 1940s.

47.1.1   Claude Flynn Howell
American, 1915 – 1997
Mending Nets, 1947.

47.1.2   Elizabeth H. Mack
American, born 1909
Autumn, c. 1940 – 47.

47.1.3   Earl Mueller
American, born 1914
Mill End.

47.1.4   Jenny Rembert
American, born 1921
Morass, 1947.

47.1.5   Mary Leath Thomas
American, 1905 – 1959
Mountain Corn.

47.1.6   Ben F. Williams
American, born 1925
Geanie, 1947.

48.1.1   Harriet Bogart
American, born 1917
Little Girl with Chicken.

48.1.2   Primrose M. Paschal
American, born 1915
Beulah's Baby, 1948.

48.1.3   John Rembert
American, born 1921
By the Winds Grieved,
c. 1940 – 48.

49.1.1   Lena Bulluck Davis
American, 1882 – 1968
Kissed by the Gods, 1949.

49.1.2   Duncan Stuart
American, born 1919
The Sisters Apollinax.

49.1.3   Gerard Tempest
American, born 1918
Leap Year, 1947.

51.2.1   Duncan Stuart
American, born 1919
Matrix.

51.2.2   Charles Sibley
American, born 1921
Set Nets, 1952.

52.6.1   Robert Broderson
American, 1920 – 1992
Quarry, 1952.

52.6.2   Jerry Caplan
American, born 1922
Carousel, 1952.

52.6.3   Roy Gussow
American, born 1918
Metaphase, 1952.

53.1.1   G. B. Chiltoskey
American, 1907 – 1973
Great Horned Owl.

53.1.2   John Chapman Lewis
American, born 1920
Night Trawlers, 1953.

53.1.3   Kenneth Ness
American, born 1903
Night Flight, 1953.

54.1.2   Claude Flynn Howell
American, 1915 – 1997
Beach Umbrellas, 1954.

54.1.3   Harry Ellensweig
American, born 1931
City Maze, 1954.

55.23.1   Margaret Crawford
American
Untitled, 1955.

55.23.2   George P. Arnold
American, born 1926
Sea and Rocks, 1955.

55.23.3   Edith London
American, born 1904
Trees, 1955.

55.25.1   Workshop of the Della
Robbia Family
Italian
*Roundel with the Emblem of
St. Francis of Assisi*, c. 1500 – 40.

55.25.2   Workshop of the Della
Robbia Family
Italian
*Roundel with the Emblem of
St. Anthony Abbot*, c. 1500 – 40.

56.28.1   Edith London
American, born 1904
Provincetown Memories No. 1,
1956.

56.28.2   Grove Robinson
American, born 1935
Regional Landscape No. 5, 1956.

56.28.3   George Bireline
American, born 1923
Painting No. 10, 1956.

57.42.1   Russell W. Arnold
American, born 1922
Painting No. 7, 1957.

57.42.2   Robert A. Howard
American, born 1922
Landscape II, 1957.

58.4.18   Robert A. Howard
American, born 1922
Landscape VI, 1958.

58.4.19 Robert Partin
American, born 1927
Behemoth, 1958.

61.2.1 Joseph Cox
American, born 1915
Yellow Wall, 1959.

61.2.2 Robert B. Dance
American, born 1934
As the Crow Flies, 1959.

62.3.1 Roy Gussow
American, born 1918
Two Forms #3, 1962.

63.13.1 George Bireline
American, born 1923
L-1962, 1963.

63.13.2 Peggie Jewell Canipe
American, born 1942
Abstraction No. 1, 1962.

63.13.5 Maggy Tamura
Japanese, born 1940
Composition with Flowers, 1963.

63.42.1 Gordon Mahy
American, born 1932
Red Table Interior, 1963.

63.46.1 Jacques Villon
French, 1875 – 1963
Hesiode, Les Traveaux et Les Jours.

64.16.1 Jean de Saint-Priest
French, 1490 – 1516
Bronze Medal.

64.28.1 George Bireline
American, born 1923
Red Shift, 1964.

65.19.1 Ann Carter Pollard
American, born 1930
The Highway, 1965.

65.34.1 Thelma S. Bennett
American, born 1910
Rain Forest, c. 1965.

66.5.1 Robert Partin
American, born 1927
Whale, 1959.

66.33.1 George Bireline
American, born 1923
Jan III, 1966.

66.33.2 Robert H. Williams
American
Poem.

67.1.1 Philip Moose
American, born 1921
On Delos, 1967.

67.39.1 George Grosz
American, 1893 – 1959
Schnee Wetter (Snow Weather), c. 1930.

67.40.1 Edgar Germain Hilaire Degas
French, 1834 – 1917
Le Repos, 1893.

67.45.2 Barbara S. Thompson
American, born 1938
Untitled, 1967.

67.50.1 Anne Hill
American, born 1932
Untitled ESCD No. 3, 1967.

68.19.1 Victor A. Pickett
American, born 1934
Double Balance, 1968.

68.33.1 Tilmann Riemenschneider
German, 1460 – 1531
Female Saint, c. 1505 – 10.

68.36.1 Unknown
European
Textile, 17th century.

68.36.2 Unknown
European
Textile, 15th century.

68.36.3/1–5 Unknown
Italian
Textiles, 16th century.

68.40.1 Dwayne Lowder
American
Variegated 3/4, 1960 – 68.

69.12.1 Alexander Calder
American, 1898 – 1976
Tricolor on Pyramid, 1965.
With additional funds from the National Endowment for the Arts.

69.13.1 Ilya Bolotowsky
American, 1907 – 1981
Open Column, 1967.
With additional funds from the National Endowment for the Arts.

69.14.1 George L. K. Morris
American, 1905 – 1975
Pieta #3, 1963. With additional funds from the National Endowment for the Arts.

69.15.1 Leo Rabkin
American, born 1919
Shadowbox-Dessau, 1967.

69.17.1 R. A. Smith
American
Impression, 1961. With additional funds from the National Endowment for the Arts.

69.19.1 Saul Steinberg
American, born 1914
Ariadne, 1966.

69.27.1 Ernest Trova
American, born 1927
The Folding Man, 1966.

69.33.1 Jacopo de' Barbari
Italian, c. 1440/50 – 1515/16
Henry V, The Peaceful, Duke of Mecklenburg. In honor of Robert Lee Humber.

69.34.1 Unknown
Greek
Torso of Aphrodite, c. 60 B. C. In memory of Katherine Pendleton Arrington.

69.41.1 James L. Burton
American, born 1940
Horizontal Light Tank, 1969.

70.31.1 Wayne Taylor
American, born 1931
Image III.

70.32.1 Jacques Busbee
American, 1870 – 1947
The Capitol, Raleigh, c. 1910.

70.38.2 Ludmila Evans
American, born 1946
Combed and Hairy, c. 1970.

71.50.1 Howard Thomas
American, 1899 – 1971
White Bridge, 1954.

72.6.1 Noyes Long Capehart
American, born 1933
Anonymous Man of the Night, 1971.

72.17.1 Sam Gilliam
American, born 1933
Untitled, 1970. With additional funds from the National Endowment for the Arts.

72.17.2 Garo Antreasian
American, born 1922
Untitled, 1972. With additional funds from the National Endowment for the Arts.

72.17.3 Richard Anuskiewicz
American, born 1930
Golden I, 1972. With additional funds from the National Endowment for the Arts.

72.17.4 Richard Anuskiewicz
American, born 1930
Golden II, 1972. With additional funds from the National Endowment for the Arts.

72.17.5 Jim Dine
American, born 1935
Paintbrush, 1971. With additional funds from the National Endowment for the Arts.

72.17.6 Jasper Johns
American, born 1930
Device, 1971 – 72. With additional funds from the National Endowment for the Arts.

72.17.7 Ellsworth Kelly
American, born 1923
Blue/Red-Orange/Green, 1971. With additional funds from the National Endowment for the Arts.

72.17.8 Matt Phillips
American, born 1927
Rocky Coast. With additional funds from the National Endowment for the Arts.

72.17.9 Clayton Pond
American, born 1941
The Kitchen in My Studio on Broome Street, 1971. With additional funds from the National Endowment for the Arts.

72.17.10 Carol Summers
American, born 1925
Tantric Landscape, 1971. With additional funds from the National Endowment for the Arts.

72.18.1 Georgia O'Keeffe
American, 1887 – 1986
Cebolla Church, 1945. In honor of Joseph C. Sloane.

73.1.1 Edith Saunders
American, born 1922
Shadows and Daisies.

73.1.2 Eleanor Davis
American, 1911 – 1985
Dahlias.

73.1.3 Eleanor Davis
American, 1911 – 1985
Beach Scene.

73.2.1 Ralph J. Cox
American, born 1944
Pink Forms.

73.2.2 Gail McKinnis
American, 20th century
Janet and the Vermeer II, c. 1973.

73.3.3 William Merritt Chase
American, 1849 – 1916
Dorothy, Helen, and Bob, c. 1904. In honor of Edwin Gill.

73.7.1 William E. Artis
American, 1914 – 1977
Michael. With additional funds from the National Endowment for the Arts.

73.7.2 Mark Tobey
American, 1890 – 1976
Picnic, 1956.
With additional funds from the National Endowment for the Arts.

73.7.3 Robert Motherwell
American, 1915 – 1991
Untitled, 1965.
With additional funds from the National Endowment for the Arts.

73.7.4/1-7 Jim Dine
American, born 1935
7 Days of Creation, 1966. With additional funds from the National Endowment for the Arts.

73.7.5 Escobar Marisol
American, born 1930
Arm and Purse, 1965. With additional funds from the National Endowment for the Arts.

73.7.6 Lee Bontecou
American, born 1931
Fourteenth Stone, 1968 – 72. With additional funds from the National Endowment for the Arts.

73.7.7 Lisa Mackie
American, born 1947
Someone was Dreaming Him. With additional funds from the National Endowment for the Arts.

74.4.1 Unknown
Far Eastern
Sarouk Carpet, 20th century.

74.8.1 Ralph J. Cox
American, born 1944
Forms on Green, 1973.

74.8.2 Eugene Berman
American, 1899 – 1972
Sunset (Medusa), 1945. In honor of Beth Cummings Paschal.

75.9.1 Maud Gatewood
American, born 1934
Out Back, 1974.

75.9.2 Walter J. Obman
American, born 1927
Nocturnal Twins, 1974.

75.9.3 Lorraine Force
American, born 1924
Rope.

75.9.4 Paul Hartley
American, born 1943
Protection VII, 1975.

75.9.5 Caroline Vaughan
American, born 1949
An Labarre, Bonnie and Jody.

75.11.1 Ralph J. Cox
American, born 1944
Forms within a Structure, 1974. With additional funds from the National Endowment for the Arts.

75.11.2 Sam Gilliam
American, born 1933
Last September IV, 1973. With additional funds from the National Endowment for the Arts.

75.11.3 Jack Youngerman
American, born 1926
Enter Magenta, 1970. With additional funds from the National Endowment for the Arts.

75.11.4/1-4 Ernest Trova
American, born 1927
Series Seventy-Five, 1975. With additional funds from the National Endowment for the Arts.

75.11.5 Gene Davis
American, 1920 – 1985
Oriole, 1966. With additional funds from the National Endowment for the Arts.

75.11.6 Helen Frankenthaler
American, born 1928
Message from Degas, 1972 – 74. With additional funds from the National Endowment for the Arts.

75.11.7 Yvonne Pickering Carter
American, born 1935
Linear Variation Series, 1975. With additional funds from the National Endowment for the Arts.

75.11.8 Anne Truitt
American, born 1921
Stone South No 36, 1975. With additional funds from the National Endowment for the Arts.

75.11.9 Ben Berns
Dutch, born 1936, active in United States since 1963
Pilot Mountain Project, 1971. With additional funds from the National Endowment for the Arts.

75.11.10 Ben Berns
Dutch, born 1936, active in United States since 1963
Pilot Mountain Project, 1971. With additional funds from the National Endowment for the Arts.

75.11.11 Ben Berns
Dutch, born 1936, active in United States since 1963
Pilot Mountain Project, 1971. With additional funds from the National Endowment for the Arts.

75.11.12 Ben Berns
Dutch, born 1936, active in United States since 1963
Pilot Mountain Project, 1971. With additional funds from the National Endowment for the Arts.

75.24.1 Claude Monet
French, 1840 – 1926
The Seine at Giverny, Morning Mists, 1897. With additional funds from the Kenan Foundation.

76.18.1 Hugo Robus
American, 1885 – 1964
Meditating Girl, c. 1962.

76.24.1 Gina Gilmour
American, born 1948
Love Letter to Lévi-Strauss, 1976.

76.24.2 Elizabeth Matheson
American, born 1942
Annapolis, 1976.

76.24.3 John Menapace
American, born 1927
Untitled, c. 1976.

76.24.4 Nona Short
American, born 1936
Vilas, N.C., 1975.

76.24.5 Unknown
Greek
Female Head (Aphrodite ?),
c. 50 B. C.

77.8.1 Severin Roesen
American, 1814/15 – 1872
Still Life with Fruit, c. 1855 – 60.
In honor of Mr. and Mrs. Charles
Lee Smith.

77.21.1 Claude Flynn Howell
American, 1915 – 1997
Nets and Ropes.

78.2.1 Howard Mehring
American, born 1931
Amarillo, 1958. With additional
funds from the National
Endowment for the Arts.

78.2.2 Louise Nevelson
American, 1900 – 88
Black Zag CC, 1964 – 71, final
addition 1977. With additional
funds from the National
Endowment for the Arts.

78.2.3 Rebecca Fagg
American, born 1950
Still Life with Gray Scarf, 1978.
With additional funds from the
National Endowment for
the Arts.

78.2.4/A-B Keith Lambert
American, born 1943
Lincoln County Landscape #2.
With additional funds from the
National Endowment of
the Arts.

78.5.1 Richard W. Kinnaird
American, born 1931
Precession, c. 1970 – 77.

78.5.2 Eric Baylin
American, born 1947
Florence, c. 1978.

78.5.3 Peter Ray
American, 20th century
Untitled.

78.5.4 Arch Johnson
American, born 1951
New Orleans 7, 1977.

79.2.1 Yvonne Pickering Carter
American, born 1939
L S D F # 50, 1979. With additional
funds from the National
Endowment for the Arts.

79.2.2 Joyce Tenneson Cohen
American, 20th century
Self Portrait (Hands), 1976. With
additional funds from the
National Endowment for
the Arts.

79.2.3 Joyce Tenneson Cohen
American, 20th century
Self Portrait (Standing at Door),
1976. With additional funds from
the National Endowment for
the Arts.

79.2.4 Joyce Tenneson Cohen
American, 20th century
Self Portrait (Hands before Face),
1976. With additional funds from
the National Endowment for
the Arts.

79.2.5 Joyce Tenneson Cohen
American, 20th century
Self Portrait (Out of Doors), 1976.
With additional funds from the
National Endowment for
the Arts.

79.2.6 Robert Rauschenberg
American, born 1925
Credit Blossom (Spread), 1978.
With additional funds from the
National Endowment for
the Arts.

79.10.1 Unknown
Greek
Athena, 300 – 100 B. C.

79.10.2 Marsha Polier
American, born 1949
Untitled # 2, 1978.

79.10.3 Robert Allen Nelson
American, born 1925
Green Powerscape, 1978.

79.10.4 Charles Springman
American, 1940 – 1986
St. Thomas Yellow, 1978.

79.10.5 Dean Leary
American, born 1944
Shell Form, c. 1978.

79.10.6 Cheng-Yi Tung
Chinese, 1900 – 1979
In the Commune Fish Pond.

79.10.7 M. Lio
Chinese
The New Look of Our Piggery,
20th century.

79.10.8 Unknown
Chinese
Horses, 20th century.

80.9.1 Unknown
Roman
Aphrodite of Cyrene, 1 – 100 A. D.

80.9.2 Unknown
German
Glass Window, c. 1500.
With additional funds from the
State of North Carolina.

80.9.3 Unknown
German
Glass Window, c. 1500.
With additional funds from the
State of North Carolina.

80.9.4 Silvia Heyden
American, born Switzerland,
1927
Jungle Flora, 1980.

80.9.5 Deborah Cofer
American, 20th century
Aunt Beebe, 1980.

83.1 Ubaldo Gandolfi
Italian, 1728 – 1781
Mercury Lulling Argus to Sleep,
1770 – 75. In memory of Robert
Lee Humber.

83.2 Ubaldo Gandolfi
Italian, 1728 – 1781
Mercury About to Behead Argus,
1770 – 75. In memory of Robert
Lee Humber.

83.6 Carolus Duran,
(Charles-Emile-Auguste Durand)
French, 1838 – 1917
Madame Carolus-Duran, 1885.
In honor of Zöe Strawn Webster.
With additional funds from the
State of North Carolina.

84.1 Unknown
Roman
*Emperor Caracalla in the Guise of
Helios*, 100 – 200 A. D.

86.1/1-2 Bamana (Bambara) Tribe
African
*Pair of Antelope Headpieces
(Tji Wara)*, 19th century.

86.3 Ad Reinhardt
American, 1913 – 1967
Abstract Painting, 1949.

87.1 Minnie Evans
American, 1892 – 1987
The Lion of Judah, 1960. With
additional funds from Mr. and
Mrs. D. H. McCollough.

87.2 Minnie Evans
American, 1892 – 1987
Untitled, 1960. With additional
funds from Mr. and Mrs. D. H.
McCollough.

87.3 Minnie Evans
American, 1892 – 1987
Day and Night, 1962. With
additional funds from Mr. and
Mrs. D. H. McCollough.

87.4   Minnie Evans
        American, 1892 – 1987
        The Eye of God, 1960. With
        additional funds from Mr. and
        Mrs. D. H. McCollough.

87.5   Minnie Evans
        American, 1892 – 1987
        Day into Night, 1962. With
        additional funds from Mr. and
        Mrs. D. H. McCollough.

87.6   Minnie Evans
        American, 1892 – 1987
        The Tree of Life, 1962. With
        additional funds from Mr. and
        Mrs. D. H. McCollough.

87.7   Minnie Evans
        American, 1892 – 1987
        King, 1962. With additional
        funds from Mr. and Mrs. D. H.
        McCollough.

87.8   Willem Buytewech, the Younger
        Dutch, 1625 – 1670
        Goats and Sheep in a Grotto,
        c. 1660. With additional funds
        from the London Memorial Fund
        and in honor of the late Mamie
        Elliot London.

87.9   Albert Bierstadt
        American, 1830 – 1902
        Bridal Veil Falls, Yosemite,
        c. 1871 – 72.

88.6/1–3 Ronald Bladen
        American, born Canada,
        1918 – 1988
        Three Elements, 1965. In honor of
        Mr. and Mrs. Gordon Hanes.

90.1   Martha Diamond
        American, born 1944
        Reflections, 1989. With additional
        funds from the National
        Endowment for the Arts and
        the Deal Foundation.

90.2   The Three Line Group
        Greek
        Attic Neck Amphora,
        530 – 520 B. C.

90.4   Moshe Kupferman
        Israeli, born Poland, 1926
        Untitled, 1974.

91.9   William T. Williams
        American, born 1942
        Double Dare, 1984. With
        additional funds from the
        National Endowment for
        the Arts.

F.92.8 Unknown
        Italian
        Frame, 1780 – 99.

92.2   Workshop of Antonio Canova
        Italian, 1757 – 1822
        Venus Italica, c. 1815 – 22.

92.9   John Singleton Copley
        American, (active in Great
        Britain from 1774), 1737 – 1815
        *Mrs. James Russell (Katherine
        Graves)*, c. 1770. With additional
        funds from the State of North
        Carolina and various donors,
        by exchange.

94.2   Yvonne Jacquette
        American, born 1934
        *Night Wing: Metropolitan Area
        Composite II*, 1993.

95.6   Unknown
        Roman
        *Head of a Woman in the Guise of
        a Goddess*, c. 1st century A. D.
        With additional funds from
        various donors, by exchange.

96.2   Gerhard Richter
        German, born 1932
        Station (577-2), 1985. With
        additional funds from the North
        Carolina Museum of Art Guild
        and various donors, by
        exchange.

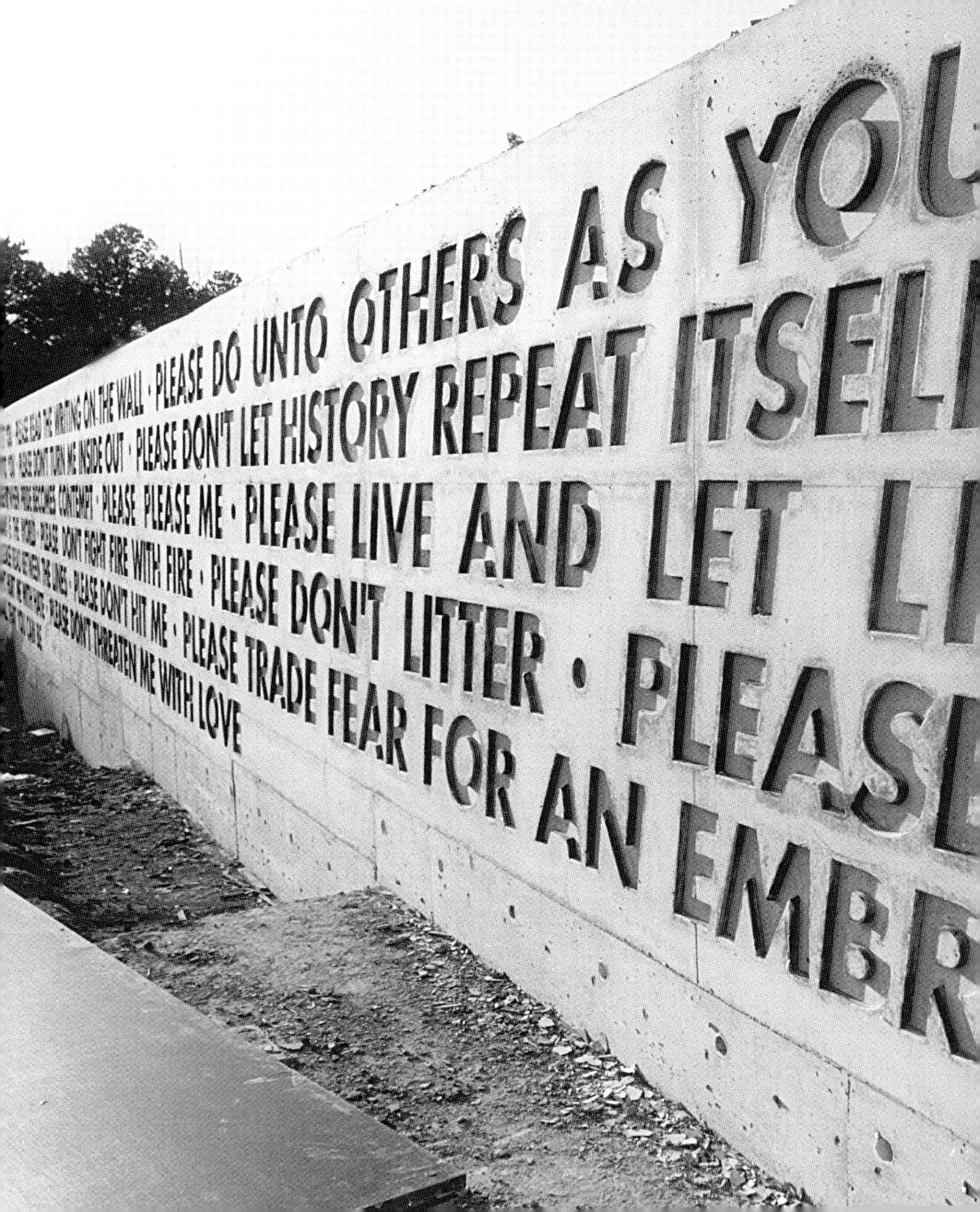
PLEASE READ THE WRITING ON THE WALL · PLEASE DO UNTO OTHERS AS YOU
PLEASE DON'T TURN ME INSIDE OUT · PLEASE DON'T LET HISTORY REPEAT ITSEL
BECOMES CONTEMPT · PLEASE PLEASE ME · PLEASE LIVE AND LET L
PLEASE DON'T FIGHT FIRE WITH FIRE · PLEASE DON'T LITTER · PLEASE
THE LINES · PLEASE DON'T HIT ME · PLEASE TRADE FEAR FOR AN EMBR
PLEASE DON'T THREATEN ME WITH LOVE

NOTES

1 Ola Maie Foushee, *Art in North Carolina: Episodes and Developments, 1585 – 1970* (Chapel Hill, 1972) 20.

2 Foushee, 26.

3 North Carolina Legislature, Chapter 314 (1929). See Appendix for the text of this legislation.

4 Paragraphs in italic type refer to art activities and events in North Carolina; however they do not relate directly to the development of the North Carolina Museum of Art.

5 Foushee, 50 – 54.

6 Ibid., 45.

7 *The News and Observer* (Raleigh, March 26, 1939).

8 Ibid., (November 25, 1939).

9 Foushee, 45.

10 "Biography of Dr. Robert Lee Humber," *North Carolina Museum of Art Bulletin*, Volume X, Number 4 (June 1971), 16–20.

11 *North Carolina Architect*, Special Issue, 20th Anniversary North Carolina Museum of Art 1947 – 1967, Volume 14, nos. 4 and 5 (Raleigh, May – June 1967), 43.

12 Foushee, 97.

13 *The Raleigh Times* (February 1, 1946).

14 *The News and Observer* (January 29,1947). Humber was quoting southern educator and humanitarian Edwin Mims.

15 Both Representative Kerr, who introduced House Bill 862, and Katherine Pendleton Arrington, the president of the State Art Society, were from Warren County, North Carolina.

16 Foushee, 110.

17 Senator Blythe was from Mecklenburg County. The first permanent art museum in the state, the Mint Museum of Art, is in Charlotte.

18 See Appendix for the text of the Act of 1947.

19 Foushee, 110.

20 Foushee, 166 – 167.

21 House Bill 1086, North Carolina Legislature, (Raleigh, April 14, 1951).

22 Foushee, 112.

23 Arrington is the president of the Art Society.

24 Gill was Director of the Internal Revenue Service, District of North Carolina and, later, State Treasurer from 1953 until his death in July 1978.

25 Poe is the senior editor and chairman of the board of the *Progressive Farmer* magazine.

26 Sommer is an art historian and a professor at the University of North Carolina at Chapel Hill. Both Katherine Arrington and Clarence Poe died while members of the commission. Sylvester Green succeeded Katherine Arrington; Egbert L. Davis, Jr. succeeded Poe.

27 Edgar Peters Bowron, "The North Carolina Museum of Art and its Collections," *Introduction to the Collections, North Carolina Museum of Art* (Raleigh, 1983, Revised 1992), XIII.

28 Foushee, 115.

29 Minutes, Board of Directors, North Carolina State Art Society (April 10, 1952).

30 Minutes, Executive Committee of the Board of Directors, North Carolina State Art Society (September 5, 1952).

31 See Appendix for a list of the works of art purchased with the $1 million state appropriation of 1947.

32 In 1953, the Board of Directors of the State Art Society authorizes the members of the State Art Commission to serve as members of the Art Society Acquisitions Committee. *North Carolina News of Art*, State Art Society — State Art Gallery, Volume 6, No. 3 (Raleigh, 1953). See Appendix for a list of purchases made in 1953 with Phifer Bequest funds.

33 See Appendix for a list of purchases made with a combination of state appropriation and Phifer Bequest funds.

34 House Bill 266, North Carolina Legislature, Chapter 696 (Raleigh, 1953).

35 Minutes, Board of Directors, North Carolina State Art Society (March 25, 1954).

36 *The Durham Herald* (Durham, North Carolina, April 7, 1956).

37 Foushee, 105.

38 *Time* (April 9, 1956).

39 William R. Valentiner, *Catalogue of Paintings, Including Three Sets of Tapestries*, North Carolina Museum of Art (Raleigh, 1956).

40 See Appendix for a list of Valentiner's gifts to the Museum.

41 *Calendar of Art Events*, North Carolina Museum of Art, Volume I, No. 2 (Raleigh, November 1957).

42 The Kress Foundation lists the *Peruzzi Altarpiece* by Giotto and his assistants, given to the NCMA, as five paintings; therefore, the total number of paintings may, in some texts,

be listed as seventy-three. See Appendix for a list of the works of art given to the Museum by the Kress Foundation.

43 Foushee, 122 – 123.

44 Minutes, North Carolina State Art Society (November 30, 1960).

45 Minutes, North Carolina State Art Society (November 29, 1961).

46 See Appendix for the text of the Kress Foundation's Indenture describing the terms and conditions of its gift to the North Carolina Museum of Art.

47 *North Carolina Museum of Art Bulletin*, Volume IV, Numbers 2 and 3 (Raleigh, 1964), 22.

48 See Appendix for a list of Valentiner's gifts to the Museum.

49 A more complete survey of these drawings is found in the exhibition catalogue.

50 Thomas J. White, "Genesis of the New State Art Museum," New Building Dedication, North Carolina Museum of Art (Raleigh, May 28, 1981), Preamble.

51 See Appendix for the names of the other appointees to the commission.

52 *North Carolina Architect*, Special Issue, 20th Anniversary North Carolina Museum of Art 1947 – 1967, Volume 14, nos. 4 and 5 (May-June 1967), 27.

53 Since 1969, the Museum has acquired 62 works of art through this program.

54 In 1972 the University of Louisville gives Bier an honorary Doctor of Human Letters; and in 1973, the Federal Republic of Germany awards him the coveted Commander's Cross for his contribution to German-American relations and his scholarship concerning the life and work of the German artist Tilmann Riemenschneider.

55 The resolution was approved by the Museum Board of Trustees and signed by Governor Robert W. Scott and former governors Dan K. Moore, Terry Sanford, and Luther H. Hodges.

56 "Landmark Dates in the Arts in North Carolina," *N. C. Insight*, Volume 1, no. 4 (Raleigh, February 1983) 7.

57 The building commission adopts the program in August 1972.

58 See the Appendix for a list of the works of art acquired with funds from the Art Society, Robert F. Phifer Bequest, through 1996.

59 In 1846, Governor William Alexander Graham ordered the volumes for the State Library.

60 The collectors gallery continues to operate until August 1982. It closes when the Museum moves from Morgan Street.

61 Thomas J. White, Paragraph 7.

62 In the Sessions of 1969, 1971, and 1973, the North Carolina General Assembly made appropriations for construction as follows: 1969, $3 million; 1971, $1 million; 1973, $4.5 million; 1974 — the second session of the 1973 assembly — $2.25 million. (Thomas J. White, Paragraph 6.)

63 See Appendix for the names of the members of the Museum Building Campaign committee.

64 *N. C. Insight*, 7.

65 Edgar Peters Bowron, "Report of the Director," A Report Covering the Period July 1, 1981 to June 30, 1985, North Carolina Museum of Art (Raleigh, 1985), 4.

66 House Bill 266, North Carolina Legislature, (Raleigh, 1952). This legislation authorizes the exchange of works of art, when, in the opinion of the Museum and the Museum Board of Directors it "would improve the quality, value or representative character of the collection."

67 *Yours to Discover*, *The New North Carolina Museum of Art*, North Carolina Museum of Art (Raleigh, 1983), 6.

68 Edgar Peters Bowron, 15.

69 The appropriation of state purchase funds to acquire works of art ranged from $10,000 in 1958 to $200,000 in 1973 and $25,000 in 1982. The last appropriation, in 1985, was $25,000.

70 "Report of the Chairman," A Report Covering the Period July 1, 1986 to June 30, 1987, North Carolina Museum of Art (Raleigh, 1987), 6.

71 See Appendix for a list of gifts from Mr. and Mrs. Gordon Hanes, the Hanes Corporation, and the James G. Hanes Memorial Fund.

72 Burroughs Wellcome has long been a supporter of the Museum. It first contributed to the capital campaign for the new building in the early 1980s. Philip R. Tracy, Jr., the company's president and chief executive officer, expressed enthusiasm for the project, saying: "Like a science laboratory, where researchers develop new ideas and inventions, *Art + Landscape* will serve as a visual arts laboratory where artists and design professionals can explore new concepts in outdoor art." [*Preview*, North Carolina Museum of Art (Winter 1991 – 92), 26.]

73 Dr. Kanof originated the Judaic collection and remains a loyal supporter of the Museum.

74 The *fin-de-siècle*, circa 1900, is a great period of Polish art history, and the National Museum in Poznan has the strongest collection of paintings from this period.

75 *Preview*, North Carolina Museum of Art (Winter 1993), 1.

76 For a history of the Kress collection, see Chiyo Ishikawa, Lynn Federle Orr, George T. M. Shackelford, David Steel, *A Gift to America: Masterpieces of European Paintings from the Samuel H. Kress Collection*, Margaret Reynolds Chace, (New York: Harry N. Abrams, Inc., 1994).

77 Egbert Davis served on the Art Society Board of Directors and the Museum Board of Trustees with Humber and became chairman of the Museum board after Humber's death in 1970.

78 See Appendix for a list of the members of the Steering Committee.

79 *Preview*, North Carolina Museum of Art (Winter 1994 – 95), 1.

80 Ibid., 3.

81 Ibid., (Spring 1996), 1.

82 Minutes, North Carolina Museum of Art Board of Trustees, Quarterly Board Meeting, September 6, 1995.

83 Ibid., November 29, 1995.

84 Raulston, also professor of ornamental horticulture at the university, was killed in an automobile accident in December 1996. His generosity will serve as another living monument to him.

85 The official dedication, scheduled for September but postponed due to Hurricane Fran, is scheduled for the spring of 1997 as part of the Museum's fiftieth anniversary celebration.

86 Kruger, an internationally acclaimed artist, collaborated on the Museum's new theater.

87 The Henry Luce Foundation of New York City awarded $70,000 to support the exhibition and catalogue. In 1993, the Luce Foundation gave $75,000 to support a two-year project to research the art and life of Mignot.

88 The Israel|North Carolina Cultural Exchange represents the most ambitious and diverse examination of Israeli art ever exhibited outside Israel. John Coffey, chair of the Curatorial department and curator of American and modern art at the NCMA, serves as director of the exchange program.

Additional Sources

Allen, Jo and Leebrick, Gil, eds., *Robert Lee Humber: A Collector Creates*, Greenville: East Carolina University, 1996.

Chamberlain, Betty, "How to Get and Spend a Million Dollars for Art," *Art News* 55 (April, 1956): 37 – 44, 95 – 97.

Crisp, Lucy Cherry, *History of the North Carolina State Art Society*. 1956.

Eveleigh, Lisa, "Private Support for a Public Collection," *Preview*, North Carolina Museum of Art (Spring, 1993): 12 – 15.

Foushee, Ola Maie, *Katherine Clark Pendleton Arrington*. Charlotte, 1986.

Masterpieces of Art: In Memory of W. R. Valentiner 1880 – 1958, Representing His Achievements During Fifty Years of Service in American Museums, North Carolina Museum of Art (Raleigh, 1959)

Upchurch, Anna, "North Carolinians Share Their Wealth," *Preview*, North Carolina Museum of Art (Summer, 1992): 8 – 10.

Upchurch, Anna, "Private Collectors Share Their Art," *Preview*, North Carolina Museum of Art (Autumn, 1992): 11 – 15.

State Art Museum Building Commission

CHAIRMAN
Thomas J. White

COMMITTEE MEMBERS
Smith Bagley
Irwin Belk
John T. Church
Egbert L. Davis, Jr.
Gordon Hanes
Gerald Arnold
Lewis R. Holding
Thomas S. Kenan III
L. P. McLendon, Jr.
Donald S. Matheson
Mrs. Dan K. Moore
Mary Semans
Charles W. Stanford

FORMER COMMITTEE MEMBERS
Hargrove Bowles, Jr.
Charles A. Cannon
Edwin M. Gill
W. Hance Hofler
Robert Lee Humber

Museum Building Campaign Fund Committee

Edwin Gill, *Honorary Chairman*
Louis C. Stephens, Jr., *Chairman*
Beth Paschal, *Vice-Chairman*

AREA CHAIRPERSONS
Henry Foscue
Seby B. Jones
Thomas S. Kenan III
Mary Semans
J. Paul Sticht
William H. Williamson III
Maurice H. Winger, Jr.

COMMITTEE
Irwin Belk
Cliff Cameron
John Church
Ivie L. Clayton
Harry Dalton
Archie Davis
Egbert L. Davis, Jr.
Katherine de Bragança Johnson
D. M. Faircloth
Thomas A. Finch
Mazie Froelich
Gordon Hanes
R. Philip Hanes, Jr.
Felix Harvey
N. P. Hayes, Jr.
Charles Hayworth
George Watts Hill
Becky Hobgood
Lewis R. Holding
Ruth Julian
E. S. Jim Melvin
Mrs. Dan K. Moore
Charles F. Myers, Jr.
George E. Norman, Jr.
Anna Ragland
Jeanne Rauch
Mrs. Charles M. Reeves
Joseph C. Sloane
Thomas Storrs
Hans Wanders

Phase One Capital Campaign Steering Committee

CHAIRPERSONS
Mazie and Jake Froelich

COMMITTEE
Anne Boyer
Ivie L. Clayton
Peggy Corbitt
Julia Daniels
John M. Dozier
Meredythe Holmes
Thomas S. Kenan III
Kay Phillips
William R. Roberson, Jr.
Terry Sanford
Charles B. Sutton
Rollie Tillman
Ann Turner

Secretaries, Department of Cultural Resources

Samuel T. Ragan, *1972–73**
Grace J. Rohrer, *1973–77*
Sara W. Hodgkins, *1977–85*
Patric G. Dorsey, *1985–93*
Betty Ray McCain, *1993–Present*

Directors, North Carolina Museum of Art

William R. Valentiner, *1955–58*
James B. Byrnes, *1960*
Justus Bier, *1961–70*
Charles W. Stanford, *1970–73*
Moussa M. Domit, *1974–80*
Edgar Peters Bowron, *1981–85*
Richard S. Schneiderman, *1986–93*
Lawrence J. Wheeler, *1994–Present*

Chairmen, North Carolina Museum of Art Board of Trustees

Robert Lee Humber, *1961 – 70*
Egbert L. Davis, Jr., *1970 – 73*
Joseph C. Sloane, *1973 – 80***
Gordon Hanes, *1980 – 87*
Charles B. Sutton, *1987 – 93*
Terry Sanford, *1993 – Present*

Presidents, North Carolina Art Society

John J. Blair, *1924 – 26*
Katherine Pendleton Arrington,
    1926 – 55
Robert Lee Humber, *1955 – 61*
Joseph C. Sloane, *1961 – 64*
Beth C. Paschal, *1964 – 67*
Katherine de Bragança Johnson,
    1968 – 70
Finley T. White, *1971 – 73*
Peggy Manly, *1974 – 76*
Sarah Reeves, *1977 – 78*
George E. London, *1979*
Ann Turner, *1980 – 81*
Mazie Froelich, *1981 – 82*
Julia Daniels, *1982 – 83*
Nancy Lilly, *1983 – 84*
Claude E. McKinney, *1984 – 85*
W. Osborne Lee, Jr., *1985 – 86*
Anne Boyer, *1986 – 87*
Roy Parker, Jr., *1987 – 88*
Lindsay Newsom, *1988 – 90*
William R. Roberson, Jr., *1990 – 92*
Peggy Corbitt, *1992 – 94*
Rollie Tillman, *1994 – Present*

Presidents, North Carolina Museum of Art Foundation

Mary Semans, *1969 – 70*
Smith W. Bagley, *1970 – 75*
Thomas S. Kenan III, *1976 – 78*
Mrs L. Y. Ballentine, *1979 – 81*
Marilyn Belk Bryan Wallis, *1981 – 85*
Mrs L. Y. Ballentine, *1985 – 87*
Thomas S. Kenan III, *1987 – 90*
Charles Lee Smith III, *1990 – 91*
Ivie L. Clayton, *1991 – Present*

Honorary Committee for
The First Fifty Years

Edgar Peters Bowron
Anne Boyer
James B. Byrnes
Ivie L. Clayton
Egbert L. Davis, Jr.
Moussa M. Domit
Ola Maie Foushee
Mazie Froelich
Mrs. Gordon Hanes
Gay M. Hertzman
John Humber
Marcel Humber
Abram Kanof
Thomas S. Kenan III
Francesca Kress
Mrs. Dan K. Moore
Beth Cummings Paschal
Marilyn Perry
Jeanne Rauch
Richard S. Schneiderman
Mary Semans
Mrs. Charles Lee Smith, Jr.
Joseph C. Sloane
Rollie Tillman
Ann Turner
Mrs. Christopher R. Webster
Benjamin F. Williams

* The Executive Organization Act of 1971 created the Department of Art, Culture, and History. The Executive Organization Act of 1973 renamed this department, the Department of Cultural Resources.
** The Executive Organization Act of 1973 abolished the Museum's board of trustees and replaced it with an art commission. In 1980, the General Assembly enacted legislation to reestablish a board of trustees as the Museum's governing body.

NORTH CAROLINA MUSEUM OF ART STAFF

Deborah H. Reid-Murphy,
Coordinator Adult Programs, 1992
Carolyn B. Fitzgerald, *Secretary,*
1990
Barbara Sills, *Slide Technician (1/2 time*
position), 1992

PUBLIC PROGRAMS

George Holt, *Director of Public Programs,*
1996
Sabrina Bailey, *Coordinator of Box*
*Office & Member Services, 1996**
H. Brooks Britt, *Park Theater Manager,*
1995
Douglas R. Champion, *Media*
Technician (3/4 time position), 1987

REGISTRARS

Carrie H. Hedrick, *Registrar, 1981*
Marcia H. Erickson, *Assistant Registrar,*
1989
Michael Klauke, *Museum Cataloguer,*
1987

Art Handling
Jay C. Schlesinger, *Head Art Handler,*
1986
James E. McKeel, *Art Handler, 1965*

Photography
William M. Gage, *Photographer,*
1989
Karen A. Malinofski, *Assistant*
Photographer, 1996
William E. Holloman, *Photo Services*
Assistant, 1986

BUSINESS AND PERSONNEL

Peggy D. Jones, *Business & Personnel*
Officer, 1974
Leslie Anderson, *Assistant, Business &*
Personnel, 1995
Allen Walter, *Office Assistant (1/2 time +*
1/2 Sec. Guard), 1994
Jeanette Holder, *Receptionist, 1977*

SECURITY AND CUSTODIAL SERVICES

Walter Jeffers, *Director of Security and*
Custodial Services, 1983
Jeanette Holder, *Receptionist/Office*
Assistant, 1977

HOUSEKEEPING

Ruby Bennett, *Housekeeping Supervisor,*
1982

Housekeepers
Gerald L. Lovett *(Medical Leave), 1996*
Malcolm L. Patterson, *1990*
David L. Perry, *1996*
Elvenna C. Campbell, *1986*
Almorine B. Brandon, *1985*
Cavazza Jones *(Temp.), 1996*

SECURITY

Michael P. DeRose, *Chief Security*
Control, 1990
Kenneth H. Smith, *Chief Gallery*
Security, 1982

Security Officers
Ralph E. Dent, *1994*
Ronald C. Hayes, *1994*
Brian D. House, *1997*
Eric Dailey, *1994*
Sylvester Stancil, *1977*
Cecil M. Jeffers, *1990*
Wilton Perez, *1996*
Gerald S. Edwards, Jr., *1994*
James O. Perry, *1984*
Robert L. Averette, *1996*

Security Guards
Peter H. Christensen, *1983*
Rita M. Elliott, *1983*
Dorina J. Marshall, *1995*
Gregory T. Davis, *1992*
Sripraphai Howrey, *1988*
Christine Bettilyon, *1993*
Michael W. Raper, *1995*
John A. Benanti, *1996*
Cathy M. MacDougall, *1994*
Sandra F. Roberson, *1976*
Paul M. Crumpler, Jr., *1991*
Carolyn L. Pfieffer, *1995*
Robert Henson, *1983*
Charles R. Fredericks, *1987*
Yong Suk Lane, *1993*
Mary B. Keeler, *1991*
Mandy G. Eaton, *1987*

Security Guards (half.time)
Allen Walter *(1/2 time + 1/2 Office*
Assistant), 1994
Edward L. Ward, *1996*
Frances M. Monds, *1989*
Mariam Cantino, *1996* **

PLANT MAINTENANCE/ENGINEERING
(Employed by DOA located at NCMA)
Julius R. Hall, *Maintenance*
Mechanic, DOA
Ralph Killette, *Electrical & Maintenance*
Mechanic, DOA
Steve Richardson, *Maintenance*
Mechanic, DOA
Garland Williams, *Maintenance*
Mechanic, DOA
Stan Young, *Maintenance Mechanic, DOA*

*   Indicates Museum of Art
Foundation position.
**   Indicates Foundation supported
state position.
All others are appropriation supported
state positions.
Dates indicate year employed.